PENGUIN
COMPASS

P9-BZJ-726

THE WAY OF THE LABYRINTH

Helen Curry, an ordained interfaith minister, Reiki therapist, and meditation group facilitator, is the founder of the Labyrinth Project of Connecticut, president of the global Labyrinth Society, and is one of the foremost labyrinth practitioners in the world. Her lectures, workshops, weddings, and other ceremonies are all part of her stated mission to "make labyrinths as common as churches and to bring spirit into matter." She lives in Connecticut with her husband and three daughters.

Helen Curry's book, The Way of the Labyrinth, *cuts a path through the mystery and intrigue surrounding labyrinths. Helen shares her journey with the labyrinth and by doing so, has created an exciting, accessible book that will answer questions about making, walking, and using the labyrinth as a ritual tool.*
—*Lauren Artress*
Author of Walking a Sacred Path:
Rediscovering the Labyrinth as a Spiritual Tool

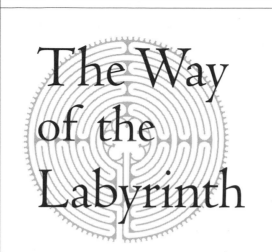

The Way of the Labyrinth

A
POWERFUL
MEDITATION
FOR
EVERYDAY
LIFE

HELEN CURRY

A LARK PRODUCTION
Penguin Compass

PENGUIN COMPASS

Published by the Penguin Group

Penguin Putnam Inc., 375 Hudson Street, New York, New York 10014, U.S.A.

Penguin Books Ltd, 27 Wrights Lane, London W8 5TZ, England

Penguin Books Australia Ltd, Ringwood, Victoria, Australia

Penguin Books Canada Ltd, 10 Alcorn Avenue, Toronto, Ontario, Canada M4V 3B2

Penguin Books (N.Z.) Ltd, 182-190 Wairau Road, Auckland 10, New Zealand

Penguin Books Ltd, Registered Offices: Harmondsworth, Middlesex, England

First published in Penguin Compass 2000

10 9 8 7 6 5 4 3 2 1

Acknowledgment is made for permission to reprint selections from the following copyrighted works:

Selu: Seeking the Corn-Mother's Wisdom by Marilou Awiakta. Copyright © 1993 by Marilou Awiakta. Used by permission of Fulcrum Publishing, Inc., Golden, Colorado. All rights reserved. • "Merger Poem" by Judy Chicago. © Judy Chicago 1979. Used by permission of the author. • *Guerrillas of Grace: Prayers for the Battle* by Ted Loder. Copyright © 1984 by Innisfree Press, Inc. Reprinted by permission of Innisfree Press. • *Peace Pilgrim: Her Life and Work in Her Own Words* by Peace Pilgrim (1983). Used by permission of the publisher, Ocean Tree Books, Sante Fe, New Mexico. • *Essene Book of Days* by Danaan Perry. Copyright 1997 Earthstewards Network Publications. Used by permission of Earthstewards Network Publications, Bainbridge Island, Washington. • *Conversations with God* by Neale Donald Walsch. Used by permission of G. P. Putnam, a member of Penguin Putnam Inc.

Image credits: page 1: Helen Curry; pages 35 and 101: Joel Berry; pages 106–9 and 113–16: Jeff Saward

LIBRARY OF CONGRESS CATALOGING-IN-PUBLICATION DATA
Curry, Helen.
    The way of the Labyrinth : a powerful meditation for everyday life / Helen Curry.
        p.   cm.
    Includes bibliographical references and index.
    ISBN 0-14-019617-X
    1. Labyrinths—Religious aspects.   2. Meditation.   3. Spiritual life.   I. Title.
BL325.L3 C87 2000
291.3'7—dc21   00-036699

Printed in the United States of America
Set in Centaur
Designed by Sabrina Bowers

For Robert, Ann, Emily, and Hilary,
and everyone who has ever had the courage
to take the first step into the labyrinth

ACKNOWLEDGMENTS

I wish to express my deepest gratitude to all of the following people, who have helped to make this book possible:

Robin Dellabough of Lark Productions for having the idea of the book in the first place, and for holding my hand through every step of the process.

Janet Goldstein at Penguin Putnam for believing in the project.

Jean Houston for graciously agreeing to write the foreword, and for rediscovering the Chartres labyrinth and introducing it to Lauren Artress.

Lauren Artress, my teacher, mentor, and friend.

Bobbye Middendorf for helping me to remember the stories.

Jeff Saward for reviewing the historical information.

Robert Ferré for teaching me how to draw a Chartres labyrinth.

David and Heidi Camhi, and Iris Archer for their thoughtful reading of the manuscript, and their moral support along the way.

Jim Sullivan for his wise counsel. My brother, Bill Post, for his invaluable advice.

Elaine Foster for helping me to create The Labyrinth Project of Connecticut, Inc., and to its past and present board members for allowing me the privilege of doing this extraordinary work.

The founding members of The Labyrinth Society for their love, support, and confidence.

From Lark Productions: Thanks to Jon Berry, Flynn Berry, Joel Berry, Lisa DiMona, Rachel Hoyt, Erin Lyons, Caitlin Stern, and Karen Watts for their extraordinary grace under pressure and hard work, both on and off the labyrinth.

CONTENTS

FOREWORD

As a young girl in New York City, I used to walk in Central Park with an old man I had met by chance. I called him Mr. Tayer, and he turned out to be Teilhard de Chardin, the great philosopher, poet, paleontologist, and mystic. The last time I saw him, in April 1955, I brought him the shell of a snail. "Ah, escargot," he exclaimed and then proceeded to wax ecstatic for the better part of an hour on the presence of spirals in nature and art. Snail shells and galaxies, the meanderings of rivers, the circulation of the heart's blood, and the labyrinth on the floor of Chartres Cathedral were taken up into a great hymn to the spiraling evolution of spirit and matter. That was how I first learned about the labyrinth in Chartres Cathedral, although it wasn't until years later that I visited there and experienced the power of that great journey in stone.

In 1962, I read a most evocative story, "Dromenon," written by the shaman-scientist-mystic Gerald Heard. It told of an archaeologist who ventured into an out-of-the-way English cathedral, walked the labyrinth incised on its floor, followed with his eyes and his fingers the same pattern carved in the walls, and through this was brought into a psychophysical state of ecstasy and spiritual awakening. The story impressed me so deeply that I adopted the image of the dromenon, the unfolding labyrinthine spiral as it is found on the floor of Chartres Cathedral, as the symbol of my work and seminars. Finally, in 1971 I visited the Chartres Cathedral labyrinth with a former Jesuit priest and theologian. We were fortunate to arrive on a day when there were no chairs covering the labyrinth, so my friend and I were free to walk it. As we progressed along the pattern of turn, my theological friend began slipping into a spiritual state of consciousness. Like the character in Heard's story, he seemed to be in a state of spiritual bliss.

I had a canvas labyrinth made and started offering walks to my students in the hope that they too would experience even a fraction of what I witnessed in my friend at Chartres. I introduced the dromenon in seminars all over the world, and soon many others responded to its sacred power and began to integrate the labyrinth walk into their work as well. One of them, Canon Lauren Artress of Grace Cathedral, studied with me for a year at my Mystery School and took the labyrinth work so much to heart that it became essential to her life and calling.

The experience of the labyrinth as I have used it had its beginning at the springtime ritual celebration in ancient Greece. Then, the *kouretes,* young male priest-dancers, performed a magical dance that had the effect of evoking a new birth in the land, in society, and in the psyche. It also marked the initiation of a second birth into a larger order. Today, the labyrinth is even more charged, more universal, mysterious, and transformative, in its use and effectiveness. It creates a sense of evolution entering into time, calling us to awaken to a citizenship in a universe larger than our aspirations and richer and more complex than all our dreams. It is the call of the larger cycle, the dance of the larger life.

Entering the dromenon summons manifold forces to the dance of one's individual life: the whirlpool, the galaxy, the whorled pattern of flowers, the very building blocks of creation, perhaps the mind of God. So it is no surprise that in many cases, especially during a ritual occasion, to walk a labyrinth brings one into exquisite states of renewed awareness, deepened consciousness, even trance.

It has been one of the pleasures of my life to offer the gift of the labyrinth to others. What is the nature of that gift? It seems to me to encompass a journey to the center of one's very being. During the walk inward, with its many surprising and disconcerting turns, one is invited to release: release old patterns, worn-out ideas and concepts, debilitating emotional memories, unhappy behaviors. Arriving at the center, the journeyer is asked to experience the recovery of her innate purposeful intelligence, one's essence. Spend time, if desired, there at the center, the still point, and know that at very deep levels, one is in union with the greatest mystery.

This centerpoint experience can range from a sense of becoming lighter, literally enlightened, to a mystical "aha!" Sometimes the joy is in silence, or a feeling of the mind/body system being rewired. One enters the doorway of a different reality almost beyond words.

For me the great work of the labyrinth is the challenge to leave the centerpoint and return outward to perform deep, loving service to the world, carrying the gifts and knowings of this visit to the heart of things.

Sometimes the results of a labyrinth encounter can be extremely practical. A student was in a very good job that would have maintained her financially for many years, but she felt she had come to the end of this career. When she arrived at the center of the labyrinth, she felt the presence of her authentic self. As she walked back out, a whole new idea of work came to her. She had recovered her profound life purpose, and went on to become an artist, which certainly paid less but which made her immensely happy.

Another student felt very depressed; in fact, he had allowed himself to fall into the habit of being depressed. We talked about the walk of the labyrinth beforehand. I explained that this was a journey of a million years. I told him of my sense that the basic turnings of the universe are circumscribed into it, and that by the time he made it to the center he would have traveled a million years. When he came back out he announced, "I don't need my depression anymore." Certainly he suffered minor bouts with it again, but nothing like it had been before.

In my yearlong Mystery School, we use the labyrinth several times. At the beginning of the term, people are asked to take on an archetype as a companion for the year. They may choose Isis, or Krishna, or Mother Mary, or some being of their own creation. They are invited to enter the labyrinth for the first time with their archetypal companion and to feel the relationship grow stronger with each turn, each step. As they travel with this mythic friend, the journey becomes mutual and the experience one of shared activation of memory, symbolic understanding, even intelligence.

In addition to the Mystery School, I have used labyrinths in weeklong seminars and in my international work. Over these past thirty years, this work has begun to assert its power all over the world. Much like an ever-widening spiral, people have embraced and disseminated their labyrinth experiences. Some have planted the many forms of the labyrinth in their gardens, or placed huge stones to mark the pattern in oak groves. The variations are great, from the seven-circle mystery found all over the world, to the larger eleven-circle version that we see at Chartres. Several times we have even created and walked it in thick snow.

In other words, labyrinths are sprouting up everywhere. What accounts for this mythic appeal? Something about the turnings of the labyrinth releases us from the tyranny of the local and the habitual. I believe that release is something we all seek. We are at a point in time in which everything is in transition, the maps no longer fit any of the territories, and the territories no longer fit any of the maps. But there are certain sureties, certain patterns in mind and body, spirit and nature, and the labyrinth is one. It allows us a map that is not a map, a journey that transcends journey, and gives a kind of clarity to our lives that we cannot find through ordinary means.

In *The Way of the Labyrinth*, Helen Curry has written a strong, cogent book that speaks to the yearnings of the age. She has provided a clear guide to the mysteries and power of the labyrinth. We can read her book and know that we are in the hands of a masterful expert who will lead us safely through the twists and turns of this marvelous journey. I especially appreciate Curry's exquisite attention to every moment of the labyrinth meditation and her insightful questions for the labyrinth walker. By combining an extensive number of blessing ceremonies with very practical advice on how to use and draw finger labyrinths, she makes the labyrinth completely accessible.

I encourage you to read *The Way of the Labyrinth* as a remembrance, as if you are remembering something that you once knew. For the labyrinth not only invites you in; the labyrinth can welcome you back to who and what you really are.

JEAN HOUSTON

PART ONE

AN INTRODUCTION
TO LABYRINTHS

CHAPTER 1

The Living Labyrinth

Where do you come from, and where are you going?
—THE RED QUEEN TO ALICE, *ALICE IN WONDERLAND*

Do you know where you're going?

We live in a society that's on the go. Everyone is in a hurry. We're forever trying to go faster. We drive to work with a cell phone wedged under one ear, planning the day ahead while wolfing down a muffin and cup of coffee. We bring computers on vacation so we can keep in touch with the office by e-mail. We have more entertainment choices than anyone has ever had in history—more restaurants, more movie theaters, more bookstores, more stores in general. We have more stuff in our homes than ever before.

And yet, like Alice, most of us *don't* know where we have been, or where we are going. We have a yearning for a greater sense of a spiritual connection, a greater sense of purpose. We see evidence of this in the newspaper, in public-opinion surveys. We read about it on the bulletin boards in health-food cooperatives and the cyber–bulletin board discussions on the Internet. We hear it in casual conversations and pastoral messages, and in popular magazines. You may see it in your own daily travels. Many of us are turning away from a life of excess in pursuit of a more meaningful existence.

The Way of the Labyrinth is a book for those of us who are looking for a tool to help us find our way. It draws on a spiritual practice that is thousands of years old and spans the world's religions, cultures, and historical epochs: walking intentionally along a path that cuts back and forth through a series of curves until it arrives at a center. No one knows for certain where the tradition of labyrinth walking began. Labyrinths have been found in ancient cultures from Greece and Crete to Egypt, China, Peru, Ireland, and Scandinavia. They can be found on the floors of great medieval cathedrals such as those at Chartres, Amiens, and Saint-Quentin in France. With roots that extend deep into prehistory, and transcending geographic and cultural boundaries, the labyrinth is believed by some to be the manifestation of Jung's theory of the collective unconscious, the sacred circle of unity. Some consider them to be magical.

In recent years, people from across the globe have rediscovered the tradition of labyrinth walking. They have recreated labyrinth designs such as Chartres's famous eleven-circuit labyrinth on canvas mats and brought them to churches, colleges, prisons, and playgrounds. They have carved labyrinths in hillsides, meadows, and backyards from natural materials such as stone or earth.

Labyrinths have been created out of nearly every material available to human resourcefulness. They have been carved on wood, on a rockface, woven into the design on a blanket or basket, laid out on the ground with water-worn stones in the desert or on shorelines or in colored stone on the floors of villas

> *Not I—Not anyone else, can travel that road for you, You must travel it for yourself.*
> —WALT WHITMAN

Interior of Chartres Cathedral.

and cathedrals, or cut into the living turf on a village green. In Roman times, the labyrinth images were crafted from mosaic tiles. The path may be planted with shrubbery, shoveled in snow, painted on cement, rolled from ribbon or rope—even outlined with plastic forks stuck into the ground, which I once did for a workshop in Lithuania. The great labyrinth on the floor of Chartres, called a pavement labyrinth, is made out of marble tiles or pavers. In New Harmony, Indiana, a replica of the Chartres labyrinth has been constructed from granite. In Naperville, Illinois, a labyrinth was laid with paving bricks.

Well over one million people have walked a labyrinth in the United States alone. There are more than 1,000 labyrinths in the U.S. today, in at least 42 states. The numbers of labyrinths and labyrinth walkers have expanded rapidly in the past decade. Hospitals, schools, churches, and corporations are building labyrinths as respite and recreation for patients, students, congregation members, employees, and clients. You can find labyrinth Web sites on the Internet, and make-it-yourself labyrinth kits are now available. Craftsmen sell small, lightweight finger-walking boards on which you trace the labyrinth's path.

People come to labyrinths for a multitude of reasons, but most find that walking a labyrinth can be a transformative experience. As people tread through the turns and counterturns of the labyrinth, the world begins to drop away. Walking, breathing, being—things that we never think about in the day-to-day whirl of life—become conscious and deliberate. The spiritual and physical merge into a walking meditation. Our pace becomes a background rhythm against which we are able to clear our minds. As one moves toward the center, one senses one is approaching a spiritual center as well. Intuition deepens. Healing occurs. Some say they hear the voice of their own truth, experience guidance, or feel a sense of grace or transcendence. Some feel they have

Roman mosaic labyrinth.

JEFF SAWARD

Marty Kermeen's paving-brick labyrinth.

brushed against the Eternal, or touched the Divine. Such experiences are the goal of any meditation, but some believe it is easier to reach them on the labyrinth than in other meditative practices.

A couple in Connecticut walks a labyrinth every year to mark their anniversary. An emergency room nurse in San Francisco finds it helps her prevent job burnout. A New York City man walks the labyrinth to bring more depth to his practice of praying. A computer analyst in Rhode Island just likes the peace and quiet. Some families walk the labyrinth together every year on important holidays, as an annual ritual. Some people walk to commemorate solstices and equinoxes and the change in the seasons. Some walk to celebrate the New Year. Some walk to reconnect with loved ones, present or not. Some walk to try to focus their energies on a problem in their community or the world—and to attempt to discern what their response to the problem should be.

Many walk the labyrinth to work on a specific issue in their life. While we often find concrete help for day-to-day concerns through labyrinth walking, sometimes the healing is much more dramatic. According to labyrinth builder and Labyrinth Society member Marty Cain, a thirteen-year-old boy who had never before spoken in full sentences described the experience of completing his first labyrinth walk in a paragraph's worth of words.

People do things on labyrinths that they might otherwise never do in public. They might step aside, smile, and greet a stranger approaching on the path; hug someone they've been at odds with for weeks; drop into a sitting meditation position or kneel in prayer to contemplate the center; recite a mantra or sing aloud.

People say they feel like pilgrims seeking truth when they walk the labyrinth. This is not new: Labyrinth walkers in the medieval cathedrals are believed to have walked the labyrinth as a symbolic pilgrimage to the Holy Land.

Solvitur ambulando, it has been said. "It is solved by walking." People all over the world are discovering that the ancient practice of walking labyrinths not only solves problems, but also soothes the nerves, calms the soul, mends the heart, and heals the body. It can help bring us into balance, giving us a sense of wholeness that is much needed for all of us whose lives ache with lopsided discomfort. Labyrinths offer the opportunity to walk in meditation to that place within us where the rational merges with the intuitive and the spiritual is reborn. Quite simply, labyrinths are a way to discover the sacred in everyday life.

The beauty of the labyrinth walk is that it is open to anyone at any stage, on any spiritual path, and from any religious tradition. It is a symbol open to your intentions. In the rhythmic process of putting one foot down, picking the other foot up, and putting it down, and in the change of turning to the left, then right, on the circuitous path, people discover the sacred within themselves. Within the energy of the twists and turns, of the going into the center and the coming back out again, people find resources within themselves that they never before knew they had.

It's one path, and whether we know it or not, all of us are on one path, no matter what religion we follow.

—Book of Reflections

Labyrinth or Maze?

When I first mention labyrinths to people, they very often think of high-walled mazes, perhaps lined with hedges. But labyrinths and mazes are not the same. Mazes are *multicursal*. You can take many paths, and there are multiple entrances. In a maze, with its blind alleys and wrong turns, you have to decide over and over again which path to take. You can get lost, disoriented, face dead ends.

Mazes are mental, linear, left-brain experiences. They force you to make choices, creating fear, confusion, or, for those lucky or skilled enough to find their way to the center, a sense of mastery or accomplishment. Mazes, too, are enjoying a rebirth—in amusement parks, hedge walks, and online and in videogames. There are even recreational mazes being created in cornfields. But they are not labyrinths.

My Journey

I've seen and experienced the power of the labyrinth in my own life. I'm a perfectly ordinary woman who has been able to use the power of the labyrinth to go to amazing places and have amazing experiences. If it happened to me, it can happen to you.

I first walked a labyrinth in February 1993, and my life changed forever. I was a suburban mom who sold insurance part-time, but I was instantaneously transformed, and labyrinths became my life's work.

In the summer of 1992, my dear friends Mary Louise Cox and Sarah Epperly invited me to help them sponsor a labyrinth walk and weekend workshop with the Reverend Lauren Artress from Grace Cathedral in San

Francisco. Dr. Artress was making her initial trip around the country introducing people to the portable paint-on-canvas Chartres-style labyrinth. In early 1993, she visited the National Cathedral in Washington, D.C., coinciding with President Clinton's first inaugural. She went on to Union Theological Seminary in New York, then came to the First Presbyterian Church in New Canaan, Connecticut.

Friday evening was to be an open walk, followed on Saturday by an all-day labyrinth workshop with Dr. Artress. I arrived on Friday afternoon, arms loaded with flowers to decorate the church. All the chairs in the church had been moved aside, and in the middle of the floor was the most astonishing, most beautiful thing I had ever seen. I will never forget that first moment seeing the labyrinth. It literally took my breath away. I could feel the most extraordinary energy emanating from the canvas and simultaneously drawing me into it. The whole experience was so profound and so moving. Something touched me like I had never been touched before.

That evening, I walked the labyrinth. I ended up walking it twice that night. During the second walk, I started to "get" the power of what this process could mean. The next day I attended the workshop led by Lauren Artress. There were about 25 people, and of those there were only one or two I did not know. Many of them were my closest friends.

It seemed to take a long time on Saturday to get to the actual walking. After an intensive introduction to the labyrinth, we approached the moment of walking it. We began with a blessing circle: We each went around the circle finishing the phrase, "I am a pilgrim seeking . . ." to help us identify the intention with which we would walk the labyrinth. By the time it got to be my turn, I was weeping. I literally dissolved in tears before the walk started, I was so utterly overcome by the beauty and power of it all.

On the walk, as we each made our way into and out of the center, our paths crossed in fascinating ways. Sometimes I found myself walking next to a friend for a while, only to discover that one of us had taken a turn, sending us off in opposite directions. Or, on my way into the center, I would meet some-one approaching me directly on my path who was on her way back out. As we came together, we would embrace, then part, and each continue on. These constant meetings and partings along the way seemed to me to be just like life. The metaphorical significance of the labyrinth and the process of walking it hit me viscerally in this first workshop, shared with people I cared for very much. It became clear to me that this process represented the cosmic meetings and partings that we all experience in life. After walking the labyrinth two times that day, I had a really strong sense that I had come Home—Home with a capital H. I had the sense that I had done this all before. I knew on a deep level that this was the work I was called to do.

The Labyrinth Project of Connecticut, Inc.

I shared with my meditation group the profound effect that the labyrinth had had on me. Several others were equally intrigued, and we decided that we would sponsor and create a labyrinth with its home base at the First Presby-terian Church in New Canaan, Connecticut. I had telephone conversations over the next several months with Lauren Artress, who was in the process of starting the labyrinth organization Veriditas as part of Grace Cathedral. I learned from her what it would take for me to do the kind of work that she was doing with labyrinths. She coached me on how to create a labyrinth and how to create my own organization.

In late August, I called a meeting for a Sunday afternoon at the church to really get the process rolling. I was superorganized—ready with agendas, job descriptions, budgets, flip charts. Not one single person showed up at the meeting. Not one. I felt literally thrown into the void. At the next meeting of my meditation group, I shared this tremendous letdown. Then the most extraordinary thing happened. All these women—completely unprompted—took out their wallets and their checkbooks and started giving me money. I left there with more than a thousand dollars, and their insistence that I just go ahead and proceed. "Who needs meetings?!" I thought.

With a press proof from Lauren Artress's labyrinth seed kit that she was about to publish, canvas from the Norwalk Awning Company, and space to paint in the Norwalk (Connecticut) National Guard Armory, we completed our Chartres-style labyrinth in two weeks in October 1993. The Labyrinth Project of Connecticut had its first public event on the solstice in December 1993, and we've been going strong ever since, with events about nine or ten times a year.

It was clearly my calling. Ever since then I've been working, living, and breathing labyrinths. I founded the nonprofit Labyrinth Project of Connecticut, Inc., and we created two portable canvas labyrinths, one a classical seven-circuit and the other an eleven-circuit (see pages 18–20 for an explanation of these terms) based on the design of the Chartres labyrinth in France. I also designed an original three-circuit ceremonial labyrinth for weddings and other celebrations at which I officiate in my capacity as an ordained interfaith minister. Meanwhile, I've been introducing labyrinths to schools, churches, community groups, and other organizations around the country, either offering labyrinth walks or running workshops. I have traveled with the labyrinth as far as Russia and Lithuania. And as part of my ongoing commitment to community service, I conduct the labyrinth walk monthly for the women inmates in the Federal Correctional Institution at Danbury, Connecticut.

*Eleven-circuit
Labyrinth Project of
Connecticut labyrinth.*

The Labyrinth Society

In 1998, I helped found the Labyrinth Society, an international labyrinth organization. The Society is dedicated to supporting all those who create, maintain, and use labyrinths and to serving the global community by providing
education, networking, and opportunities for transformation. We have over
200 members worldwide from the United States, Great Britain, Canada, Aus-
tria, and Singapore. It is a fertile and heart-opening organization, full of the
most incredible people who are passionate about all aspects of labyrinths. We
welcome people from both the Christian high church labyrinth tradition, as
well as those who come to labyrinths from the earth energy traditions, includ-

ing dowsing, healing, art therapy, paganism, and others. If you want to connect with the Society and its members, locate the labyrinths they have created, or find related books, newsletters, and labyrinth Web sites, you can go to the directory and resource sections on pages 217–50.

Through *The Way of the Labyrinth,* I want to introduce the labyrinth-walking meditation to as many people as possible. I truly believe that the rediscovery of the labyrinth can help us positively transform our world.

Your Journey

You may have a passing familiarity with labyrinths. Perhaps you've walked one, or know someone who has. You may find something in the image itself that resonates in you and intrigues you, and you want to know more: You long to have the labyrinth whisper its secrets in your ear. Or you may be exploring ways to enhance your existing meditation practice and see the labyrinth as another tool.

No matter what you bring to the book, and no matter what brought the book to you, *The Way of the Labyrinth* is a journey of joy and empowerment. I will explore what labyrinths are, where they come from, the different kinds and ways to make them, and how others have used or responded to labyrinths. I will focus on contemporary uses of the labyrinth and how this symbol from the deep reaches of our past can be a path to healing, balance, and ultimately to a sense of spiritual wholeness. I will draw on others' stories, which have come to me from the *Book of Reflections,* the guest book maintained by the Labyrinth Project of Connecticut. While there is an outward journey in the discovery process—getting to know and experience the labyrinth through walking—more crucial is the journey inward. It is this, your personal journey, that I am privileged to facilitate by describing the wonders of the labyrinth.

The labyrinth is a useful metaphor for many of life's journeys: getting married, having children, seeking an education, earning a livelihood, identifying a spiritual path, achieving world harmony. No matter how lost you may feel, in a true labyrinth you are never lost. You are exactly where you are supposed to be. The labyrinth can create a state in which problem solving, either conscious or subconscious, can occur. Labyrinth walkers, in my own experience, have received invaluable help with many life transitions as well as everyday issues—everything from reducing stress, grieving the loss of loved ones, completing a doctoral dissertation, resolving sleep disorders, running board meetings, dealing with a mastectomy, and deciding on a career move, to connecting with the creativity and enhancing mental energies and alertness. If you pay attention as you walk, you can find out a tremendous amount about yourself. You can quiet your mind for reflection, inspire your creativity, or help prepare and nourish yourself for all parts of life's journey.

By trusting the process of the labyrinth, of putting one foot in front of the next, you can travel a long way. I know this experientially from the labyrinths I have walked. One word at a time, and the book is written. One foot at a time, and the journey is accomplished.

Whether you are "walking" a finger labyrinth or the 40-foot terrazzo labyrinth outdoors at Grace Cathedral, the walking meditation consists of three main parts: walking toward the center, being in the center, and walking back out. By learning about the three parts and how they differ, you will find you are able to walk even more mindfully. Through the stories, you will come to understand how the labyrinth fulfills the deep need humans have for simple rituals and for connection with both mind and heart, right brain and left brain. I'll also explain how to build a full-scale labyrinth in your garden or public park.

The Way of the Labyrinth teaches you everything you need to know to incorporate labyrinth meditation into your own life. The book shows you how to apply

I felt lost and then found myself again and again— beautiful journey.
—BOOK OF REFLECTIONS

this ancient remedy to modern challenges. We each come to the path bringing our many realities, our individual histories, the unique journeys we have traveled. To experience the labyrinth is to acknowledge that the paths merge. In our fractured and fragmented world, this metaphor can set the stage for powerful healing energies on many levels—within individuals, communities, and nations. With love and blessings, I wish you Godspeed on your journey.

Preparing the labyrinth.

JOEL BERRY

LESSONS FROM THE LABYRINTH

"A dozen or more people are walking in socks on a forty-foot canvas painted in the ancient pattern of the labyrinth at Chartres Cathedral. I join them, feeling the unexpected hard bricks beneath my feet, their softened and worn edges outlined through the canvas. As I encounter my first person walking out of the labyrinth, I wonder how we'll get around each other on the narrow path, outlined in purple. He steps aside without fuss and I pass. The next person turns sideways, and the next touches my hand. I continue, realizing that I can't tell whether the older man walking on a parallel path is on his way in or out of the labyrinth. I wonder how far it is to the center. When I do reach the middle, several people are sitting down in traditional meditation poses. A young woman stands to pray. A white-haired woman raises her arms in a joyful gesture. I take a moment at each of the six petals, considering first the kingdom of rocks and minerals; second, the kingdom of plants; third, the kingdom of animals; fourth, the human estate; fifth, the angels; and sixth, the Ultimate Divine. It helps to consider each in turn, to acknowledge each and give it its due. I start my walk back out, feeling a connection to those coming in and my fellow walkers on the path back to the mouth. This time, I step aside as an older man approaches his journey inward. Our eyes meet. His smile is so sweet it hurts. By the end, a half-hour later, I know I've undergone an opening, an illumination of the soul. I feel different, changed in a way that I can't adequately describe. And all because I put one foot in front of the other, effortlessly following an age-old path."

—BOOK OF REFLECTIONS

CHAPTER 2

The Ancient Labyrinth: History and Meaning

*Arise! Watch. Walk on the right path. He who follows the right path
has joy in this world and in the world beyond.*
—THE DHAMMAPADA

What makes a labyrinth? They come in all different shapes and sizes. They can be as small as the labyrinth that appears on the cover of this book or smaller, like the labyrinths that were placed in the margins of medieval texts. The labyrinth of Chartres Cathedral is 40 feet across. I have built labyrinths that are 80 feet in diameter, and others have built even bigger ones. Some labyrinths have a "classical" design: a clean, simple path with an equal number of turns and counterturns. Others take their form from nature.

For all their differences, labyrinths share common elements. The most im-

Labyrinth at Sneinton, England.

JEFF SAWARD

portant is that they are "unicursal," meaning "a single course or path." Once in the labyrinth, you need only follow the path. There are no dead ends in a labyrinth. There are no choices to make to take this or that direction. You cannot get lost in a labyrinth. If you stay on the path, you will arrive at the center.

Labyrinths are often described by the number of "circuits" they have. "Circuit" is another word for the number of circles or rings that comprise a labyrinth, not including the center. The Chartres Cathedral, for example, is an

Coin from Knossos with circular labyrinth.

JEFF SAWARD

eleven-circuit labyrinth. Many labyrinths are "seven-circuit" and others are "three-circuit."

The opening through which labyrinth walkers begin their journey is called the "mouth" or entrance. The walkway or trail of the labyrinth is the "path." The sides of the path are the "walls." The parts usually are strategically placed, and have an internal symbolism. The Chartres labyrinth, for example, is divided into four quarters; each quarter has seven 180-degree turns.

The circular path of the classical labyrinths is also significant. The labyrinth is part of a tradition of symbols involving circular movement, including Sufi dancing and sacred circle dances from all over the world. The labyrinth is part of the canon of archetypal symbolic circles of meaning—including wholeness, unity, and the divine center in cultures around the globe and in every period from prehistory to the present.

The Santa Rosa Labyrinth©, by Lea Goode, Labyrinth Society member, is a contemporary labyrinth design using seven circuits, equal-armed quarter markings, and a small space on the fourth path where no one walks. This heart-space is approached from all four directions and can be used for contemplation while traversing the labyrinth.

No one knows exactly where the labyrinth originated. The eleven-circuit labyrinth of the Chartres Cathedral, while reproduced all over the world and perhaps the most familiar image in the history of labyrinths, is only a relatively "recent" example—one of the "revivals" of labyrinths throughout time. The truth is that labyrinths are much older. Labyrinths have been traced to the cradle of Western civilization in the Mediterranean. A famous classic seven-circuit labyrinth has been found on coins from Knossos, Crete, from three centuries before the birth of Christ. The coins—some of which show circular labyrinths, others of which are square—are believed to refer to the mythological labyrinth of King Minos, in which the Minotaur was kept.

It's likely, though, that labyrinths are older, perhaps much older. According to Jeff Saward, Labyrinth Society member and editor of *Caerdroia*, a British journal devoted to the study of labyrinths and mazes, a clay tablet from Pylos, Greece, containing the design of a labyrinth is 3,200 years old. A Syrian pot shard showing a labyrinth is believed to be of similar vintage. A seventh-century B.C. wine jar from Tragliatella depicts armed soldiers on horseback riding from a labyrinth that has the word "Truia" (Troy) inscribed in the outermost circuit.

Archaeologists have found what we have come to call the Greek key pattern on artifacts whose dates preceded ancient Greece by thousands of years.

LEFT: *Syrian pot shard.* RIGHT: *Seventh-century wine jar.*

Greek key or meander symbol.

Anthropologist Marija Gimbutas found a meander pattern on a figurine in the Ukraine that dates from 18,000 to 15,000 BCE. She also found it in a bird goddess figurine from the Vinca culture in what was northern Yugoslavia. If you take the Greek key symbol and rotate it outward, it becomes a labyrinth. Many believe the root of the labyrinth pattern derives from the shifting, twisting path of the Meander River of Phrygia in the Mediterranean region of present-day Turkey. (The word "meander," or to wander aimlessly, was derived from the same river.) The word *labrys*—which means "double axe" and is believed to be the root of "labyrinth"—comes from the same region. Prehistoric labyrinths, carved on rockfaces at Pontevedra, Spain, are probably from the early Iron Age (ca. 750 B.C.). At another prehistoric labyrinth, Naquane, in Val Camonica, Italy, a pair of eyes is carved in its center so that it looks like a face.

The labyrinth symbol was widely adapted by the Romans (there are numerous examples of the design in mosaic pavements) and transported throughout the Roman Empire from Britain to Eastern Europe to North Africa. Some Roman labyrinths, marked on the ground, were ridden on horseback as a test of skill. Turf labyrinths, formed by turf ridges and shallow trenches leading to a small mound at the center, have been found throughout Europe. These classical, seven-circuit labyrinths were often called "Troy Towns," or "Walls of Troy," in homage to the famous walled city. In Wales, their name "Caerdroia," or "Walls of Troy," also meant "city of turnings." In Scandinavia, more than 500 stone labyrinths, mostly near what used to be the coastline, have been recorded. Similar labyrinths have also been found in Russia, Iceland, and the Baltic countries. Labyrinths were painted on church walls throughout Scandinavia.

Labyrinths have been found far afield from Western civilization as well. Stone labyrinths have been discovered in India. In China, ca. A.D. 1000, labyrinths were constructed out of incense for keeping time in ceremonial

Turf labyrinth in Great Britain.

rituals. At the corner where each path turned, a different incense scent started. You could literally smell what time it was!

Individual labyrinths have their own internal symbolism. The labyrinth at Rheims was located in the same place within the cruciform cathedral as those at Chartres and Amiens. If one sees the building as Christ on the cross, this would put the labyrinth at his knees. The knees are ruled by Capricorn, and according to the Church, Jesus was a Capricorn.

Labyrinth researcher and my fellow Labyrinth Society member Sig Lonegren has theorized that the animal labyrinths of the San Jose Pampa near Nasca, Peru, were totems or "power animals." He believes they were walked as a ritual for empowerment, with the goal of the walker to gain, or to take on, the power of that particular animal. The labyrinths are believed to have been constructed about A.D. 500. They were brushed onto the unbelievably dry, flat ground of the desert. Many of these magical, single-path tools were "mirror" patterns, meaning that you walked on the line, not the path. The labyrinths reflect an incredible attention to detail. In the spider labyrinth, Lonegren notes, the opening is on the right of the spider—the leg that carries the spider's eggs, the source of "fertility, reproduction, and continuation of the species." You literally enter and leave the labyrinth through the source of the spider's power.

The Tohono O'odham and Pima tribes of southern Arizona wove baskets with labyrinth images from dried leaves, stems, and roots of desert plants. The labyrinth, known as the House of Iitoi, symbolized the pathway to the top of Baboquivari, a sacred mountain. Iitoi was the tribes' ancestral founder whose spirit resides at the top of the mountain. From time to time Iiotoi's spirit would sneak into the village; he escaped by confusing people with the deceiving twists and turns of the trail home. On the path to the center of the labyrinth one can see Iitoi and trace the mysterious and bewildering journey leading back to the peak of Baboquivari.

JEFF SAWARD

Nasca monkey.

*O'odham Indian basket
(man in the maze).*

JEFF SAWARD

There is a good reason labyrinths have endured for many centuries. They offer a special kind of spiritual balm and symbolism not available in anything else. Robert Ferré, director of the St. Louis Labyrinth Project and another Labyrinth Society member, says, "Walking the labyrinth is another way of tapping into forces beyond our normal conscious mind. It takes us to some ancient part of ourselves, as old as the turning of the planets and stars, as old as the goddess and earth energies, back when night was dark, when people knew the sky and nature was a part of us and we of it. This is something lost in our modern world, and the imbalance that it causes cries out for resolution. That's why the labyrinth touches so many people so forcefully."

As many stories are told as mythologies exist, but whether in spiritual or secular use, the labyrinth seems to represent a path to be followed, however long and difficult, to reach the center, the object of the journey. We have precious few records about the specifics of how labyrinths were used. Part of the magic of the labyrinth is that no one knows its origins, nor are there clues as to how the same symbol came to flourish in cultures widely separated in time and space. But many stories have been passed down through the generations. They suggest that ancient cultures walked the labyrinth for good fortune, protection, connection with the sacred center, pilgrimages, healing—reasons that resonate with us today.

Good Fortune and Protection

Throughout Scandinavia and around the Baltic Sea are stone labyrinths near what used to be the shore of the sea. According to scholars, fishermen seeking a good catch walked these labyrinths. Walking or running the labyrinth was believed to be beneficial to collecting strong winds. Bad omens—bad weather and evil spirits—could be lured into the labyrinth and left there. Trapped in its curving coils, they could do no harm. Wives of fishermen would run the labyrinth when bad weather approached and the fishermen were out on the water, to propitiate the storm energies—drawing them away from the boats and into the labyrinth where they would do no harm. The oldest of these labyrinths have been dated to medieval times. But the practice of walking labyrinths for good luck persisted among fishing villages into the twentieth century.

Lapp hunters and shepherds in Finland would also walk the labyrinth for good fortune. The protection they sought was from wolves, wolverines, and trolls and other evil spirits, which they hoped would follow them into the labyrinth and be unable to find their way out from the center.

Ancient labyrinths were often associated with protection, guarding that which was central or sacred to the community, such as cities, places of worship, sacred mountains, or important buildings. Roman mosaic labyrinths were surrounded by fortified walls, protecting the center of the labyrinth and the cities of the Roman Empire. A painted labyrinth threshold design in India was known as a *kolam*, or fort. The idea of protection connected labyrinths with the walls of the great ancient city of Troy—giving rise to the name "Troy Towns" or "Walls of Troy" for the turf labyrinths of Europe.

The labyrinth symbol was also used near doorways by the Romans throughout their empire, presumably for protection. And according to scholar Maxine Kaltenmark, in Taoist texts of ancient China, sacred caves were considered labyrinths. At the center was often a great treasure, such as a sacred teaching or text.

The Hero's Journey

Perhaps the most famous labyrinth story in Western culture is the Greek story of Theseus, Ariadne, and the Minotaur. According to the myth, the architect and builder Daedalus built the labyrinth for King Minos of Knossos on the island of Crete. At the center of the labyrinth was a half-man, half-bull creature known as the Minotaur. Minos had the labyrinth built after his son died while visiting Athens. As tribute, every nine years the Athenians had to send their seven most esteemed young men and seven loveliest ladies to Minos. The fourteen were paraded before the crowds when they arrived and then sent into the labyrinth. When they arrived at the center, they were consumed by the Minotaur.

Theseus, son of Aegeus, the king of Athens, persuaded his father to let him be part of one of the groups that was to be sent to be sacrificed to the

Minotaur. Theseus enlisted Minos's daughter Ariadne, who had fallen in love with him, to help him. He trailed her magic thread behind him to the center of the labyrinth. There, he destroyed the Minotaur. Then, following the magic thread, Theseus found his way back out and escaped with Ariadne and his fellow Athenians. At the first stop on the way home, the island of Delos, Theseus, Ariadne, and their fellow travelers performed a dance called the Gerano, or Crane, Dance, which was said to be a reenactment of their torturous journey in the labyrinth. (The mating dance of the crane apparently is similar to the back and forth rhythm of walking a seven-circuit labyrinth.)

Images from the story traveled throughout Europe. The famous Cretan coin depicting a labyrinth is believed to refer to the labyrinth of Knossos. In many cultures, "crane dances" are danced as part of labyrinth rituals. In Slupsk, Poland, on an enormous turf labyrinth 150 feet in diameter, as part of an elaborately complex costumed festival, dancers would tread the "lapwing step" around the coils of the labyrinth. The dance was based on the crane dance. The myth even found its way into Roman graffiti. Scholars studying a house in Pompeii, Italy, the town destroyed by the volcanic eruption of Mt. Vesuvius in A.D. 79, found the words *Labyrinthus Hic Habitat Minotaurus,* or "The Labyrinth, here lives the Minotaur," etched into a pillar—apparently a warning to steer clear!

The Cycles of Life

Throughout history, the labyrinth has been a symbol of the cycle of life. Labyrinths have been associated with childbearing. The famed Chartres Cathedral labyrinth may have been used as a birthing instrument. It's made of 272 stones, the average number of days in human gestation. Perhaps these labyrinths were walked to achieve good fortune for the child's life, or as a meditation on the process of birth and renewal. Among the Hopi, the labyrinth, as a representation of new life and reincarnation, took two forms—one circular, one square. The circular "Tápu'at," or Mother and Child, is a labyrinth within a labyrinth. The shape represents the unborn child within the womb and the child cradled in its mother's arms after birth. The mother and child represent the rebirth from one world to the succeeding one, symbolized by the emergence itself. The labyrinth is the female womb; it can only be entered if one is pure and perfect. The other (square) labyrinth is the Sun Father, the giver of life. The male figure represents the human seed, which can penetrate the womb and produce new life—a new birth or reincarnation—and eternal life.

In China, according to Maxine Kaltenmark, labyrinth themes, including the related motifs of meanders, caves, spiral towers, shells, and pearls in Taoist texts, are often linked to the themes of life, death, and resurrection.

Many believe that labyrinths were walked as part of funerals, part of the process of letting go of departed loved ones and connecting and reconnecting with the spirits of those who have gone before. The labyrinthine path guarded the center where the souls of the dead ancestors resided, barring them from escaping and causing trouble in everyday life but making them contactable once the labyrinth had been traversed. Some ancient labyrinths in Sweden were located high up in hills and mountains associated with ancient graveyards. The labyrinths probably were thought to be the homes of the ancestors' spirits. One labyrinth, at Låssa, in Uppland, Sweden, was built in the middle of the grave field; the burial sites were in the cairns and mounds alongside the labyrinth.

The Feminine Center

Earth Mother. Birthing instrument. Birth and rebirth. In labyrinth rituals across cultures, women were literally at the center. Stories abound from Scan-

The labyrinth is the feminine face of God.

—BOOK OF REFLECTIONS

dinavia and Britain of community festivals and dances featuring the classical seven-circuit labyrinth with a lovely maiden in the center and races by the young men to see who could get to her first. An eighteenth-century document records that at the turf labyrinth in Saffron Walden, England, young men would challenge one another to run the labyrinth to reach the young women who would stand at the center.

Many scholars believe that labyrinths originated in goddess-worshipping cultures. Some speculate that Bronze Age Crete, the land of King Minos, was among the last strongholds of a goddess-worshipping civilization. Similarly, Troy—commemorated in the "Troy Town" labyrinths across Europe—is also viewed by some as the last bastion of a goddess-centered culture. Ariadne, in the story of Minos's labyrinth, may be viewed as an actual goddess—the woman with the thread, the answer to how to get to the center of the labyrinth and then back out.

The Labyrinth as Christian Allegory

The Christian world's use of labyrinths was ushered in during the Middle Ages. Manuscripts began to depict labyrinths in the margins. The symbol connoted a passage that was important but difficult to get into and out of, or to comprehend. Other texts placed labyrinths at the end of manuscripts, or on maps to note the location of Crete. The great tradition of labyrinths in medieval Christianity, though, was in their use as a symbol for pilgrimages. Early Christians took a vow to make a pilgrimage to Jerusalem to walk in the step of the historic Jesus. When the Crusades made the actual trip too dangerous and expensive for the European pilgrims, massive cathedrals were designated pilgrimage shrines throughout Europe. Labyrinths were constructed as part of the pilgrimage. The cathedrals at Chartres, built in less than thirty years around the year A.D. 1200, and Amiens are two of the prime examples. Chartres still has its original labyrinth today and Amiens has a reconstruction. Smaller labyrinths were also placed at the entrance of many churches, probably for seekers to trace with their fingers before entering the sacred space. Thus the labyrinth was used as a symbol of Christian faith, the one true path to eternal salvation.

Within those cathedrals, the labyrinth pattern embedded in the stone floors of the nave became the final steps of the pilgrim's journey, which was often taken on the knees in worship. The journey symbolized the twists and turns of life as well as an unmediated experience of the mystical itself, a torturous pathway that could not be traversed without the support of the church. In this final leg of the journey, Christian pilgrims took the symbolic trip to the center to touch the divine. It is easy to believe that these religious pilgrims felt much less separation between body and soul than we do today. They not only accepted the world around them—and the connection between the body, land, and the cycles of nature—but they also opened their hearts to the truths of the divine on such pilgrimages under the close watch of the mother church.

About three centuries ago, labyrinths fell out of favor in the church. At Chartres, the labyrinth was covered with chairs. Other labyrinths in the great European pilgrimage churches built at the height of the Middle Ages fared less well. They were literally torn out of the floor. Some researchers point to practical considerations for the shift. The labyrinths at Rheims and St. Omer in France are said to have been removed because they encouraged noisy behavior among children, which disturbed worshippers. Some church labyrinths had a history of being used for dances and games as well as worship—an uneasy balance that many contemporary churchgoers might relate to. Others point to the influence of the scientific revolution, which led to a weeding out of older, "pagan" traditions.

It's possible that labyrinths raised thorny theological issues as well. The solitary experience of the lone pilgrim walking the labyrinth, in an allegory of the religious life, could also be seen as an invitation to a direct experience of the divine. Many religious leaders distrusted such experiences, believing that it was necessary to have mediators—the priests—between the worshipper and the sacred. They did not believe that individuals were able to truly discover, encounter, and comprehend Truth on their own. It is a matter that some religions, centuries later, continue to struggle over.

Labyrinths Today

Good fortune. Protection. Empowerment. Spiritual insight. Connection to the earth, to nature, to the eternal. The reasons that the ancients walked the labyrinth are still relevant today. This may be part of its allure. In walking it, you are following the same path—the same walking with intention to the center and back—that others have for thousands of years. You become one with the pilgrims of the Middle Ages; with the people of San Jose Pampa in Nasca, Peru; with fishing communities in Scandinavia; with lovers in ancient Greece; with Theseus and Ariadne.

Labyrinth revivals spring up with startling intensity at varying times and locales throughout recorded history. Why should that be? More and more historians, archaeologists, and ethnologists are studying this question and pursuing labyrinth research. Perhaps scholars will uncover the answers to the unsolved questions of the labyrinth. Perhaps not. The labyrinth may remain an enigma, cloaking its origins and connections in the veil of mystery it has woven for thousands of years. Perhaps ultimately its message to us will be that all that really matters is what each new generation brings to the process of walking. In finding "the right path" that the *Dhammapada* prescribes, we find the joy that is meant for us. The labyrinth flourishes anew.

PART TWO

WALKING THE
LABYRINTH

CHAPTER 3

Preparing to Walk

All journeys begin with a single step. All adventures begin with fear.
Within the unknown is understanding. Each day is the beginning
of a season of growth for each of us.
—BOOK OF REFLECTIONS

First things first: How do you find a labyrinth? Check the Labyrinth Directory on pages 217–43 and Recommended Resources on pages 244–50, including the Web sites of labyrinth assocations such as the Labyrinth Society or Veriditas, where members list their labyrinth walks, events, and newly created labyrinth installations.

Perhaps you are in an area where there are no public labyrinths or no regularly facilitated walks or workshops. This may be a temporary situation, since labyrinth walking is undergoing a grassroots revival around the world. New labyrinths are being built and installed all the time, all over the country and all over the world. Labyrinth maker Robert Ferré and others are keeping busy these days: St. Louis–based Ferré and his staff alone are creating several new labyrinths every week.

I predict labyrinths will be available almost everywhere in the very near future. Those of us involved in the work see healing potential as labyrinths pop up in hospitals, prisons, schools, churches, retreat centers, parks, playgrounds, gyms, even parking lots: anyplace where people gather. In addition, a full, significant experience is always available with finger labyrinths (see chapter 8 for a detailed discussion).

Once you gather the basic information, you will need to find out if there are walks scheduled at particular times. Is the labyrinth open to the general public with no restrictions? At the Labyrinth Project of Connecticut, we offer walks approximately every six weeks, on a specific evening. The First Presbyterian Church of New Canaan is our home base, but the labyrinths are not available at all times. At Grace Cathedral in San Francisco and at St. James Cathedral in Chicago, there are outdoor labyrinths open and available to walk 24 hours a day year-round.

You'll want to know if the labyrinth you are going to is outdoors or indoors. Is it a permanent installation, or has a labyrinth been temporarily installed for a special event? If the labyrinth is indoors and painted on canvas, you will be asked to remove your shoes and wear only socks. Many portable labyrinth facilitators offer walkers a basket of socks to put on. However, if, like me, an insole or arch support is necessary for your comfort while walking, you might bring you own indoor slippers. Sometimes walking without the usual support of shoes can be difficult for people, and depending upon the kind of surface the labyrinth is placed on, it may also be hard underfoot. Be prepared to accept this as part of your experience.

No matter what labyrinth you are using—whether it is a full-size labyrinth

Shoes off for the labyrinth.

JOEL BERRY

or a finger labyrinth—there are three parts to the journey. The first is the pathway into the center. The second is the center itself. The third is the pathway back out of the center. The third part of the journey is actually the same pathway as the first part, but with a crucial difference. You are walking in the opposite direction to crate a symmetrical, balanced experience.

There is a tradition, with its roots in the earth labyrinths of Sweden on the Baltic coast, of people running as fast as possible through outdoor classical labyrinths. Then, there are people who come to the walks I facilitate and spend the entire evening—three hours—walking the two labyrinths. There are people whose very intense concentration on each footstep means that they take a long time to do the walk. One very athletic-looking young man stays the whole night at our walks. He is like a dancer or a Tai Chi master: Each slow, stylized step reflects his meditation. He has set aside the entire evening to complete this short journey.

While I tell people to allow at least an hour to meditate and walk both labyrinths at the Labyrinth Project of Connecticut, I also encourage people to let go of their sense of time and time constraints as they walk. How long it takes will depend, too, on the size of the labyrinth. Walking the 80-foot out-door Chartres-style labyrinth I built in a meadow at a very slow pace would take an excruciatingly long time. But again, the amount of time it takes to walk is not the point. I want people to stop thinking about the labyrinth walk as something to be done with a stopwatch. It is a chance to step out of linear time and into the timeless. Who can say how long that really takes?

What to Wear

An important consideration when you are dressing for a labyrinth walk is your comfort. You don't want to wear clothes that interfere with your ability to concentrate on the walk. As with other meditation practices, there are those for whom wearing something special, some item of clothing specially reserved for labyrinth walking, helps them get into the meditation more easily. If you find that meditative activities are enhanced by specific ritual or costume, then by all means wear something personally unique and significant for your labyrinth walk.

The bottom line for clothes is, anything goes. Over the years, I have seen walkers in everything from black tie and evening dress to cutoffs and T-shirts. Blue jeans are probably the most popular item of clothing, closely followed by business suits and sweat suits. Sometimes there will be a lady walking in a feathery boa, or someone bedecked with multiple floating scarves. A tremendous positive energy can result from making fabrics available as part of the walk. Some labyrinth facilitators regularly offer baskets of thin, large squares of beautifully colored silk or nylon that people can drag behind them like a train, fling over their shoulders like a cape, wrap themselves in, or turn into veils or turbans. It can be quite dramatic.

The visual sweep, the foot-eye coordination of the labyrinth did some truly amazing things to my brain senses. I see what a heavy burden my impatience is.
—BOOK OF REFLECTIONS

LESSONS FROM THE LABYRINTH

At New Year's Eve labyrinth walks, people are generally dressed in their most festive outfits, such as black tie and evening dresses, because they are headed off to a fancy party afterward. We sometimes have kids in pj's—I used to bring my youngest daughter to my evening walks in her pajamas on a regular basis. I remember one woman walking in her floor-length black coat. She was very thin. As she walked the twists and turns of the labyrinth, I was aware only of this long black coat going around and around and around. Another wonderful costume was a blue cloak with a hood worn by a good friend in the early days of the Labyrinth Project. As my friend walked, she put up the hood and covered her head. I was taken back to medieval times as she walked the turns of the pathway while holding a tall wooden staff as a walking stick. The image of ancient pilgrimage that the costume brought to mind conjured for me a sense of homecoming of déjà vu.

The Benefits of Preparation

Like every journey, the journey of the labyrinth depends on what you bring to it. It can be enhanced immensely by advance preparation, a sense of openness, and reflection afterward. The first time some people walk a labyrinth is like a dream. Effortlessly, they drift into a meditative state. Their body's rhythms—pace, breathing, thoughts—quickly settle and instinct takes over. They know what to do when someone approaches—when to smile, when to make eye contact, when to exchange greetings, when to step out of the way. Insights bubble up from their subconscious. Problems that they have struggled over begin to seem less insurmountable. It is as if they have been given a gift from God.

For others, the labyrinth is a challenge. They wonder what brought them there. They fret about doing the wrong thing: Will they make a wrong turn? Will their efforts to greet someone seem like an intrusion on their meditation? Will the problems of day-to-day life—the shopping that has to be done, the doctor's appointment that needs to be scheduled, the personal question that has been vexing them—keep them from reaching the state of grace that others find on the labyrinth? Will they look silly? Will their labyrinth walk be a failure?

Why do some people find fulfillment on the labyrinth and others disappointment? Why do some people have rich, meaningful walks time and again? The labyrinth itself is only a pathway. It is paint on canvas, stones on the ground, a pattern in mosaic. The power of the labyrinth, as with any spiritual practice, is in what you bring to it. The labyrinth is a portal, a door to spiritual growth. But you have to know how to open it—or "gnow" how to open it, in the gnostic sense of immersing ourselves in this mysterious process of winding toward the center and winding our way back, as labyrinth researcher Sig Lonegren says. The labyrinth is a path to connect you to the still, small voice, the sacred within yourself.

Preparation for a labyrinth walk can itself be an intense meditative experience as well as simply enhancing the actual walk. Your preparation may start before you leave home or even when you are just entertaining the idea of going on a labyrinth walk. Even to go into the walk consciously aware of your intention, "I want to try this *just because,*" can create an opening.

Without some degree of mindfulness and conscious intention, walking a labyrinth can lose its meaning—or never achieve a meaning. Any form of preparation will increase the benefits, and will help you slip more easily into walking the labyrinth on future occasions.

Start with Attention

Most excursions are more enriching if you can put yourself into a mind-set of enthusiasm and anticipation. If you allow yourself to become rattled by changes, upset about the unexpected, or panicked at the thought of being out of control, even the best of voyages is likely to find you in a state of frenzy. On the other hand, if you are open to experience, you might arrive for your journey ready to accept and relish all that comes your way.

Before you take your first actual step on the labyrinth, try to be in a state of mindfulness; be present in the moment and pay *attention*. It is important to apply both your mind and your heart. You need to consciously observe what is going on within you and around you as you follow the labyrinth.

How do you achieve this state of attentiveness? For some people, it just happens. As they begin to walk, the everyday melts away into timeless bliss. Others have told me they have been able to reach a state of perfect pitch while a part of their mind is pondering the mundane, such as what to have for dinner or whether or not it's time to rotate the tires on the car. This doesn't happen to me—at least, it hasn't to date. I need to work to reach a state of mindfulness, whether in labyrinth walking or other spiritual disciplines. I have to find ways to shut myself up if I am to have a chance at prayer, meditation, or insight on the labyrinth.

For some people, a simple mantra can help. Others say that mantras get in the way, that they can achieve a better meditative state without any words, perhaps with an image or a particular focus. I have often taken the suggestion from the Buddhist author and spiritual leader Thich Nhat Hanh to focus all my attention on the soles of my feet. You can use the image of moving away from the old and into the new with every step of the journey. Or you can simply align the pace of your walking with the pace of your breath. If, like me,

The thoughts of everyday stop, blissfully.
—BOOK OF REFLECTIONS

holding a phrase in your mind—a meditation or a mantra—is what will help you move across the bridge into the numinous, you'll find suggestions on pages 49–51.

Your Intention

The most powerful influence you can create for your labyrinth experience is your *intention*. You may not be able to achieve complete attentiveness. Something going on around you or in your life may distract you, even momentarily. But you do have complete control over your intention. You decide what your intention is for the labyrinth. You choose it, you state it, and you become it. While you refer to it as you walk the labyrinth, it is not necessary for you to keep restating your intention. It is with you.

The intention of your walk can grow out of any number of areas: meditation, spiritual transformation, worship, ceremony, psychological growth, stress reduction, healing, grieving, family issues, problem solving, team building, leadership development. Stop and consider what is on your mind. If seeking a change is one reason to walk a labyrinth, think about what kind of change it is that you seek. Having a clear idea about the change you want to make will help you create an intention that will yield the result you want.

Take a moment to consider how your intention can inform the concept of the three parts of the labyrinth: the path in, the center, and the path out. Also consider how the three-part experience can enrich and enliven your intention. The more aware of this you are as you are walking, the more open you will be to the richness of the pilgrimage.

In the Christian faith, there is a tradition of dividing spirit into three parts—Father, Son, and Holy Spirit. You might consider the three persons of the Godhead as you follow the labyrinth path, focusing on God the Father,

Enlightenment for a split second is far better than no enlightenment at all.
—Book of
Reflections

manifesting Divine Power or Divine Will on the way into the center. At the center, experience the Holy Spirit as Divine Breath, Inspiration, or Wisdom. Focus on the Divine Son, the epitome of Divine Love manifested in the world, as you take your path back out. Others from a Christian tradition might simply experience each step on the path as traveling with Christ along the way.

In the Episcopal tradition, a sacrament is defined as an outer manifestation of an inner grace. For me, walking a labyrinth often has a sacramental feeling to it, although it isn't an officially ordained sacrament of the Christian church, such as baptism, marriage, or holy communion. It helps to think of walking the labyrinth as though it were a sacrament, an outer symbol of an inner grace.

Thinking in terms of the three parts of the Self (conscious, superconscious, and subconscious) is another fruitful way to enrich the labyrinth experience. You could decide consciously what you want your intention to be, focusing your conscious self on that intention as you follow the pathway in. At the center you become aware of the superconscious or divine realm influencing that intention. On the walk out, you might enlist the help of your subconscious to bring your intention into the world.

You may not come up with an intention easily. Whenever I find that I am having trouble focusing on an intention, I go back to the imagery of pilgrims. It was the very first intention I ever experienced in labyrinth walking. We were told to complete the phrase "I am a pilgrim seeking . . ." I have found over the years that focusing on what you are seeking brings an intention to mind clearly and quickly. If you know what you want you can usually describe it. This advice has never failed to guide me to exactly the intention that I needed.

*I am
a pilgrim
seeking . . .*
—COMMON
LABYRINTH
INVOCATION

Shedding Expectations

One caution on intentions is that they do not become expectations. It may seem like an overly subtle distinction. It is not. An intention is a way of being.

You might say, "My intention for this labyrinth walk is *to be open* to receiving *guidance* about this question." Expectations, on the other hand, are tied to outcomes. You have an expectation when you say you want an "answer for a question." Expectations set you up for disappointment. They can lead to failure. They don't allow for the unexpected, the insight that surprises. To expect something is to wait in anticipation for it to happen to you, and then to pass judgment on it. If you expect to receive a specific answer to a specific question and you don't get one, you may be disappointed. If you expect to react in a certain way and find you are reacting differently, you may think, "I must have done it wrong." If you expect to receive a blinding insight and you don't get one, you may think that you didn't deserve to "get it." Your attitude may be "Go ahead, make my day" as you sit back, crossing your arms. The labyrinth doesn't work that way. Any expectation that you may have of how it will or should be will automatically get in the way of your ability to fully participate in how it really is.

I know. I've been able to walk with intention, being truly open to the labyrinth and being given an insight that I had not previously been open to. And I've also had the misfortune of walking the labyrinth with expectations. It is possible to stay so focused on your expectation that you don't even recognize what you are given in the experience of walking the labyrinth. I have seen countless people over the years come off the labyrinth in a state of astonishment. They went into their walk expecting one thing and they ended up getting something completely different.

A labyrinth walk can set into motion many different thought patterns, emotions, energies, ideas, and questions, none of which may lead to insights or answers immediately but which may eventually produce transformations long after the walking meditation has been completed. So don't fall into that expectation trap of thinking that if you don't receive insights right away, nothing happened. Some things take time.

LESSONS FROM THE LABYRINTH

At the start of one labyrinth walk I asked myself what it was that I was seeking. I for-mulated my intention, but it seemed like an overwhelming goal: I was seeking guidance on how I could secure release from an anxiety about a particularly difficult relationship that had been troubling me for some time. I spoke my intention: "I am a pilgrim seeking release from this anxiety." I did not have any idea how this might happen and oddly did not feel any particular attachment to the outcome. I had grown weary of worrying about it. It had been gnawing at me, and I had been gnawing at it for long enough.

I started out on the labyrinth walking at a comfortable pace and concentrated on letting go of extraneous thoughts. I repeated my intention one more time, putting all of my concentration into the desire behind the words. An extraordinary thing happened. I had the awareness of picking up my left foot to take the next step forward. When I felt it hit the floor again I had an instantaneous sense that the anxiety I had been feeling about the relationship was gone, released, over and done with. I kept walking. I felt like I was the same person. I hadn't changed, yet I felt completely different. I tried thinking about the person who had been causing me the pain. I realized that I couldn't change her and, amazingly, that I didn't need to. Yes, we would continue to disagree about many things, most things, in fact, but I knew then that we would find a way to work it out.

It was miraculous. In the space of one step I had walked out of one world and into another without even breaking my stride. In stating to myself that I was a pil-grim seeking release from the anxiety, I was articulating, probably for the first time, that I was ready to let go of it.

I wish I could say that all of my labyrinth walks are like this. But they are not. I've learned the hard way not to let myself be overtaken by expectation. I learned one of my most memorable lessons on labyrinths and expectations as I was walking an outdoor labyrinth that I had created for the Dominican Sisters' Retreat Center in

Saugerties, New York, in a meadow overlooking the Hudson River. It was the first outdoor labyrinth that I had ever made, 80 feet across, double the size of the famed original one on the floor of Chartres Cathedral. The pathways were grass and the "walls" were made of bricks which had been dug into the earth at ground level and laid end to end, so that the whole labyrinth could be mowed. Because the labyrinth was so large and so flat, one could look across the meadow and not even see its farthest pathways.

A year after I finished it, I came back on a chilly spring afternoon in the expectation of having a wonderful, bucolic walk. With only birds for company, I planned to give myself over completely to the full experience of peace and tranquility, joy and enlightenment that I knew would be mine in this environment, which was perfect for a walking meditation.

I began the walk, settling into an easy pace, enjoying the rhythm of the movement. But as I rounded the first turn I began to feel uneasy. By the time I had rounded the next couple of turns I had the extraordinary sensation that I was lost. The pathways did not seem to connect with each other. Surely I would never get to the center and the experience of peace and tranquility that I believed was "mine."

I started to panic. Had I made a horrible mistake laying out this labyrinth? Would all the time and money spent literally sinking the labyrinth into the ground turn out to be a huge joke, sending people endlessly around and around in circles and never bringing them to the center? I started running to reach the center and prove myself wrong, or right—I wasn't sure which. My rational mind knew that not only had I created this labyrinth correctly, I had successfully walked it upon its completion. But I couldn't see the end. Because of the size of the labyrinth, and how it had been laid out, I could only see the path immediately in front of me. I felt truly shaken.

Finally I got to the center. All was well. I had fallen victim to my expectations. I stood in the center and laughed out loud at myself. It had been so ridiculous— where was my trust in the process?

Later, on reflection, I came to understand and appreciate the lessons I had learned. The first lesson was to let go of expectations. The second was that, even after years of working with and creating labyrinths, I still could not begin to understand the power and the complexity of the labyrinth experience.

Choosing a Meditation

After your intention, the next element of a labyrinth walk is choosing a meditation. While it is perfectly acceptable to walk with a clear and open mind with no mental images or words, many people find it difficult to do, especially in the beginning. As a technique for reducing the mental chatter that plagues most of us, a meditation or a mantra can be repeated along the way.

You may wonder why I do not suggest using your intention as the meditation or the mantra. There is no reason why you can't. I don't because it usually doesn't have a rhythm that is conducive for walking. In addition, chanting your intention through the entirety of the labyrinth walk may place too much emphasis on the intention. See what works for you.

I use a meditation that is in alignment with my intention for that particular walk.

I try to synchronize my pace so that each word or syllable of the phrase is equal to one step. Sometimes I am more successful than others, but having the mantra always in mind helps me to stay focused on the walking instead of on the other things that can creep into my consciousness.

What you want to have on the tip of your tongue is a phrase that will mirror your intention and inform the pace of your walking. "Be still and know that I am God," from Psalm 46:10, for example, always has an instantly calming effect upon me. Often I find that I am almost humming it as I go along. Sometimes I get only as far as "Be still and know," other times only to "Be still," or even just "Be." It doesn't matter; the effect is still the same. It begins to pull me out of my everyday consciousness and into that state of meditation that is the goal of my labyrinth walk.

Toning, or using the voice as an instrument for creating vibrations of sound through the whole body, can be effective as well. A mantra as simple as the classical Sanskrit "Om" captures the alpha and the omega—the beginning and the end—and it can become your mental/vocal equivalent of wholeness.

If my intention for a particular walk is to gain some form of strength or guidance, I might choose "I will look to the hills from whence cometh my help." If I am seeking a new direction in my life or taking on a new task, I might choose the prayerful "Lord, make me an instrument of thy peace," from St. Francis. Or if I want to gain a broader perspective, I might remember a favorite or particularly meaningful children's song—"Row, row, row your boat gently down the stream . . ." for example. Today, if I were walking a labyrinth, my meditation would be the Buddhist prayer "Let love, compassion, joy, and peace encompass the whole universe."

Choosing Meditations for the Moment

If you seem to be coming up empty in selecting a mediation, and are looking for some good source, consider the following.

Every faith's holy book is a rich source of wisdom to use on your walks: the Bible, the Torah, the Koran, the Bhagavad Gita, the Upanishads, the Yoga Sutras, the Dhammapada, the Tao-Te Ching, or the sayings of Confucius. Collected works of the mystics from different faiths, such as the Philokalia, the Greek Orthodox texts of mystical wisdom and practice, also offer wonderful sources for exploring and discovering meditations. Zen koans are deceptively simple. Other sources for meditations might include the verses of Sufi poet Rumi, the thoughts of the Dalai Lama on ethics and happiness, inspirations from Buddhist author Thich Nhat Hanh, the collected words from the wisdom traditions of the world in the works of Eknath Easwaran; Huxley's *The Perennial Philosophy; Women in Praise of the Sacred*, edited by Jane Hirshfield; and the rich contemporary work of Neale Donald Walsch in the three volumes of *Conversations with God* and *Friendship with God.*

There are wonderful pocket anthologies of short prayers or meditations. Some focus on a single tradition. Others share the wisdom insights from many traditions. At the end of the book, I include other resources that I have found an inspiration over the years.

Random Selection

For those who prefer a more secular mantra, selecting a single word to meditate on can prove a useful way to go deeper.

When I do the prison ministry, I sometimes take a bag of meditation cards called angel cards. This pack has a single word on one side of each small card: ADVENTURE, PLAY, GRACE, HOPE, ABUNDANCE, TRUTH, HARMONY. Each inmate can pick a card out of the bag and carry it with her on the walk, allowing that word to inform her walk for that day.

Another idea is to use the dictionary. Close your eyes. Flip the pages back and forth, let it fall open, and, still with eyes closed, bring your finger to the page. Then open your eyes. Whatever word you've landed on is the one that will offer the deepest meaning for your explorations on this walk. Simply working with that "random" word—(assume it was not an accident, whatever word your finger landed on!)—go deeply into thinking about that word, how it affects your life, what it means to you now, what it may mean after the walk, how its meanings and ramifications can be present with you on the walk and on the path back out. You may be surprised how prescient the seemingly random word can be, and how much meaning you can draw from it.

"What Should I Think About?"

This commonly asked question is really less about "thoughts" than about "fear"—fear of failure, fear of not knowing, fear of the unknown. The question assumes that there is a right and a wrong way to walk a labyrinth. It as-

---

LESSONS FROM THE LABYRINTH

"For the walk, I selected a word from the dictionary, a random word. What was amazing to me was the word that I got: Believe it or not, my finger randomly landed on 'Peace.' All I could say was, 'Wow!' Here I was in this state of being totally stressed out—way too much to do, too many irons in the fire, jobs, kids, husband, burnout on the near horizon. Yet when I selected a word at random, I came up with 'Peace.' It seemed like the ultimate message to me at this moment in my life. I asked myself what else could I possibly need, once having gotten this incredibly powerful message. So I took that word on the walk with me that night. I'm no Pollyanna, and I have no way of knowing if everything will turn out all right, but somehow in that space, I did experience an inner peace that has been missing in my life for years— even decades. I almost can't believe that I got this message, but I did. Maybe I will have to consider the possibility of there really being angels."

—BOOK OF REFLECTIONS

sumes that the seeker does not know the difference between the correct and incorrect way but an expert has the answers. Finally, it assumes that there is nothing wrong in giving away the power of one's thoughts to another who knows better. Nothing could be farther from the truth.

This kind of thinking stems from our analytic left-brain training. In linear and logical learning, there are "right" answers and "wrong" answers. We all strive to be "right" because coming up with the "wrong" answers usually results in some negative consequence. We are not steeped in the right-brain traditions of the labyrinth, in which intuition and whole-brain thinking lead you. The labyrinth taps wholeness and intuition so that, through the walk itself, you learn that there is no right or wrong way to do it.

To ask what you should think about is to miss the point of the labyrinth. It is a tool for you to know your *own* truth.

Taking a Measure of Your Feelings

Taking stock of how you are feeling before the start of your journey enables you to compare it with how you feel at the end. If a labyrinth walk is a pilgrimage or a journey with an intention that holds the potential for change, how will you measure this change if you don't know where you began? You bring your entire being along for the walk. It is important to gauge where you are in each aspect of yourself. So take a moment to check out how you are feeling and what emotional luggage you may be bringing along with you.

After you have focused on how you feel in your physical body—your mind, your emotions, and your spirit—think about whether there is a relationship between the intention that you have set for your walk and how you are feeling. If there is no connection between the two, you might want to consider revising your intention to bring it into alignment with how you are feeling. For example, if you are feeling very tired, your intention might be to be open to a shift in your stamina. Or you might say that you are now ready to let go of the experience of feeling fatigue. Remember not to frame it as an expectation.

As you prepare, ask yourself where you are in the overall process of labyrinth walking: Are you a beginner? Have you done it before and want to go deeper? Are you looking to enrich an already-established part of your meditations? Where are you as you anticipate this particular labyrinth walk?

To some degree or another, you have now considered what you want to focus on in your life and have created your own idea about why you might be doing this labyrinth walk. You have set your intention for the walk. You have chosen the meditation or mantra that you will use to carry you forward. You have taken note of how you are feeling. You are ready to begin the journey. Into the labyrinth you go!

A Guided Meditation
for Preparing to Walk

"How to Labyrinth" is a series of sections like the audio tapes you rent at a museum for expert guidance to the history and highlights of a painting or sculpture. In these sections I will be your tour guide for walking the labyrinth.

Focusing Your Attention

The first step of any labyrinth walk is an inward one, taken before you ever make a move: "being simply and fully present. This is perhaps the most important aspect that you need to experience for the labyrinth to function in its highest and best level. At the very least, before you take the first step, you will want to touch the inner stillness, and use your preferred method—if you have one—to turn off the brain chatter. Maintaining attention—whether you call it "mindfulness," as does Jon Kabat-Zinn in his book *Wherever You Go There You Are,* or whether you consider it "heartfulness," as does *Artist's Way* writer and author Julia Cameron—can be a challenge.

For some, the mantra or the walking meditation phrase can help create the transmutation from everyday life to mental sacred space. For others, only silence or perhaps music, or the focus on a single mental image, will be effective. Experiment to see what is going to work best for you. And remember that each walk is different. You may find having a variety of techniques to draw on will allow you the utmost flexibility in getting what you need from each labyrinth walk.

Setting Your Intention

Your intention can be anything you want it to be as long as it is authentically yours. You might want to hold a question or an issue in your mind. You might choose "to walk with an open mind and an open heart," or it might be "just for the fun of it." Whatever spontaneously comes to mind is fine, just as it is okay to ponder something that you may have been working on for a long time.

Shedding Expectations

I suggest that you leave *all* of your expectations behind as you enter this pilgrimage. One of the most useful ways of shedding expectation simultaneously leads to a potentially powerful intention. It can be simply to admit that you don't know: "I came not knowing what to expect," or "I didn't know why I was coming here." In explicitly stating that you don't know, you are honoring the possibility of discovery without attaching an expectation to it. That is actually a very effective place to be, particularly if you can let go of any judgment about not knowing. Let it be okay that you don't know.

Remember to pose intentions as requests for guidance or insights, not as answers, so that you are not setting yourself up for unfulfilled expectations. Shedding expectations helps you remain open to the unique gifts that each labyrinth walk offers.

Taking a Measure of Your Feelings

How are you feeling physically right now? Do you have lots of energy? Are you tired? Are you experiencing any pain? If so where? Do you know why? (There should not be any more physical strain associated with labyrinth walking than there is with any other kind of walking.)

Ask yourself how you are feeling mentally and emotionally. Are you excited, nervous, bored, impatient, happy, depressed, at ease? Are you comfortable with how you are feeling right now? If not, why not?

Finally, can you gauge where you are spiritually? Do you feel a connection with the Divine in your everyday life? Can you see the Divine in others and yourself? What is your idea of spirituality, anyway?

Questions for the Journey

If you don't already have one, consider getting a special notebook just for your labyrinth meditations and reflections. Consider writing your answers to these questions as part of your preparation process every time you go on a labyrinth walk.

1. Why am I doing this labyrinth walk?

2. What is my intention?

3. What will my meditation or mantra be?

4. How am I feeling before I begin?

5. What baggage am I bringing along with me?

6. Do particular questions of my own come to mind as especially important for me to address? (List them here.)

CHAPTER 4

On the Way In

There is no such thing as an incorrect path—
for on this journey you cannot "not get" where you are going.
It is simply a matter of speed—merely a question of when you will get there.

—NEALE DONALD WALSCH
CONVERSATIONS WITH GOD

You stand ready, poised at the entrance to the pathway. When you enter the labyrinth and take that first step, it might feel more like a leap of faith. What is it about first steps that give them such weight? This is a journey through the paths of a particular labyrinth. More importantly, it is a journey into your own inner being. That may be the scary part. You do not necessarily know what is there, what you will find or discover along the way. You may think that you do not know where you are going, or how you are going to get there. It helps to remember that this experience is about trusting the process,

Stone labyrinth in Copenhagen.

JEFF SAWARD

and trusting yourself. Know that all you need to do is to put one foot in front of the other and you will get to the center of the labyrinth—and to your own center—and back out again.

The way into the center is often seen as a time of anticipation or an opportunity for preparation. You have already considered letting go of things no longer needed. You have gone through a period of preparation before taking your first step. Yet "preparing" for the center is something that you do at each step along the pathway in as well. Each review of intention; each moment of attention to your walk, your physical body, your emotions, your slowly quieting mental chatter; each repetition of the mantra or meditation serves to take you deeper through the turns, deeper into your inner world. Another useful image for your walk in is that of moving away from the past and into the future. There is often a sense of making yourself ready to receive that which is to come.

As you begin to feel a pace appropriate to the particular labyrinth walk, your movement can help to bring brain and body together. These two long-estranged parts of ourselves yearn for union and wholeness, even if we don't always know it. The labyrinth walk, with its constant turns, speaks the language of movement. On this self-contained, inner-directed circular path, body and mind can meet. What do they have to say to each other? You have an opportunity to listen to the dialogue that may be generated.

One woman recounted a very concrete and vivid interplay between the physical and emotional planes: "At first I felt very unsure on my feet, because I was recovering from an ankle injury. I also felt uncomfortable as I touched those that passed, and afterwards I reflected on how that is true in my life—that I am shy and tend to get uncomfortable when other people touch my life or try to. I had a great sense of anticipation for getting to the center. At times it was difficult to stay present. I liked that I could stop and rest. That helped to ground me and rest my ankle, and gain my strength for continuing on. It's interesting that my job was supposed to have ended several times in the last month, and just two days before [the walk] was officially my last day. I am being laid off and will be entering a new path, which is full of excitement and fear and the known and the unknown. It was good timing that I was able to walk the Labyrinth. It was a great ritual for me to 'start on a new path' with all the aspects I experienced there, and to be able to come to the center and be one with God and the universe."

Another young woman once told me that she was the shyest, most insecure and self-conscious person she knew. When she finally got up the courage to pass the man ahead of her on the labyrinth walk, she felt she had claimed her right to be who she wanted to be. She had been working on being more assertive for a long time. The labyrinth helped her to solidify a dramatic change that she had been working on. It seemed to happen all of a sudden, right in that moment. She experienced profound and practical results.

Woman and three boys on the way in.

That is why the labyrinth is a metaphor for life. If you pay attention to how you are walking, you can learn a great deal about how you live.

Rules of the Road

The number of rules for walking the labyrinth is nowhere near the number of rules of the road for driving your car. There is really only one rule, which is to walk at your own pace. It is fine to stop along the way; just remember to be respectful of others and their space as you meet or pass them on the path. When it is crowded, it is all the more important to stay true to your own inner voice while interacting with compassion with every other pilgrim along the way.

I remember from a workshop years ago the comment that if everyone walked labyrinths there would be fewer car accidents! Why? The point was that through walking the labyrinth, people would all learn to honor each other's right to be on the path. It would serve to make drivers more polite about making way for others to merge or to offer the right-of-way at stop signs. Unfortunately, I have observed that feelings of road rage are more common than you might think—even on the labyrinth. This unwholesome trend seems to have permeated all parts of our world.

There is virtually no wrong way to move through the labyrinth. I have seen people dance, run, crawl, walk backwards, and try it with their eyes closed. There is no need to turn a labyrinth walk into a somber occasion. It is perfectly okay to have fun. When walking in a group, be respectful of other people's space and their right to a meditative walk. Within those broad guidelines, just about anything goes.

I had one woman crawl the path on her hands and knees, and someone else traversed the path belly-down. The rules of the road would have you walk around such pilgrims. Or, if your own pace is sufficiently slow and deliberate, you could certainly continue on the path behind the person. As in life, it is okay to pass someone ahead of you who may be going slower than you would like. If you have been to the center and are on your way back out, I suggest you step aside on the pathway for those who are coming toward you and who are on their way in. This is to keep the inward flowing energy moving, but it is not a hard and fast rule.

Once someone starts walking, try not to interrupt him or her—the whole point is for all to walk at their own pace. The proviso here is that one should not unduly inhibit other people's experience. I grant you that can be a fine line, and where it sometimes gets hard for me. I don't like to police someone's walk.

My body couldn't wait to get started. I felt an undeniable urge to place my belly on the labyrinth and crawl belly-down and so I did.

—BOOK OF REFLECTIONS

I always err on the side of not intervening. I have never walked onto the canvas and told someone that they are being inappropriate, neither at a workshop nor at a walk. The most intrusive I have ever been as to tell some people *behind* a slow-moving pilgrim that they could go around.

Feeling the Path

"I followed my slow-moving husband," wrote one woman after her first labyrinth walk. "I would have preferred to walk more quickly, and, as in most of my meditations, my thoughts were flying all over the place. I was distracted by the noise that my husband's new corduroy pants were making and stifled my laughter. Rule number one: Don't wear new corduroy pants to a labyrinth walk. . . . I glanced up at a banner that read *Rejoice.* My eyes forever went to it after that. Standing at the mouth of the labyrinth, I had posed a question before entering: *What would you have me do with my life?* I got no immediate insights except the ever present word on the banner."

She concluded by saying, "I truly feel the message that I learned from the labyrinth walk was to let go of many of the rules I have placed on myself and my life, to slow down and to rejoice. Rejoice and be released from this labyrinth of my own design."

The pathways of a labyrinth can be thick and rich with input for the senses, a veritable marketplace of sights, sounds, smells, sensations, jostling, movement, meetings, partings, negotiations, energies, things seen and unseen, things felt and unfelt, things brought along and things left along the way. Labyrinths can be containers for all of human experience. Like a ride in a crowded subway car, we rarely emerge completely unaffected or unscathed by the closeness of such an encounter with other beings. For some, such close proximity to others in sacred space can cause discomfort. Especially for those

LESSONS FROM THE LABYRINTH

"I only wish life could have the same rules as the labyrinth. I wish we could all really go at our own pace. If we all could relax and slow down once in a while, or speed up and pass others if we wanted, then maybe we'd all get to wherever we are going right on time, and receive what's there for us to receive, and give in return. I wish life could just be much more like this—one slow walk.

"I noted that people walked on the labyrinth so differently. Whether with their heads up, down, straight ahead; their hands in their pockets; their arms by their sides, behind their back, or in front of them; or whether they swaggered or strolled, I realized it doesn't really matter, because no matter what, they're all walking on the same path that starts from the same place and ends up in the same place."

—BOOK OF REFLECTIONS

more accustomed to solitary meditation, the initial labyrinth walk can be disorienting. As one first-time walker put it, "Never having been in a labyrinth, I panicked when people started coming at me. Wrong way? Then I realized that wherever I ended up or what I did was the right way for me!"

It's important to honor whatever you are feeling. I love how Neale Donald Walsch puts it in his book *Conversations with God:* "Feeling is the language of the soul." If it's giggles over corduroy pants, then let it out! The labyrinth is about the path to accepting your own authenticity. The only kinds of thoughts that I don't recommend are: *I am going to do this quickly. I'm going to stand up straight. Even though my hip hurts, I am going to smile.* Labyrinths offer you an opportunity to accept rather than deny what is real about yourself.

I walked the
labyrinth
feeling others'
joy and
sadness as well
as my own,
and
understanding
that I didn't
have to fix the
others' pain or
add to their
joy, only
validate and
allow their
feelings.

—BOOK OF
REFLECTIONS

One great lesson that I have learned from the labyrinth actually took place when I wasn't even on it. I was outside the labyrinth observing at one of our public walks when I became aware of a woman who was wearing pink slacks and walking at a snail's pace. Being a born New Yorker, I was fascinated that anyone could move so slowly and still be moving at all. A long line of people quickly formed, all moving just as slowly behind her. Very soon, I became disturbed by this situation. So I silently sent a telepathic message to the first person behind her to go ahead and pass.

But the telepathy didn't work. The line of barely moving beings was getting longer and longer. It was driving me nuts just to watch it. Why weren't the others passing her? Unable to contain myself, I walked over to my friend Elaine, nodded toward the labyrinth and the barely moving pink legs, and whispered, "What are we going to do about this?"

"I don't think there is anything we can do." She smiled back at me. I went back to my spot and waited. Nothing happened.

Finally, I couldn't take it any longer, so I quietly moved nearer to the edge of the labyrinth, ready to catch the eye of the first of the followers when they rounded the next turn. The moment came. I leaned forward and in a loud stage whisper said, "You know, it's okay to pass!" The response was only a solemn nod. No break in the agonizingly slow forward movement, no change in posture, no change in the pace.

And then I got it. What kind of control issues did I have about how people walked "my" labyrinth? Sure, go ahead, walk at your own pace, but make sure that it's okay with me how you do it! The message could not have been clearer, swifter, or closer to the mark. And boy, did I need it! I do not know anything that is so efficient as the labyrinth for this kind of teaching, if we will only pay attention to it. My only regret was having to interrupt someone's deep meditation in order to learn it.

LESSONS FROM THE LABYRINTH

"I've come to the labyrinth twice in my life, both times at a crossroads, and I came away again with the strength to go with the truth—the truth to myself. The peace I feel as I walk back out from the center reaffirms my soul." A friend going through a major life transition wrote this. She had worked for many years at the same company, itself a rarity these days. But the changes afoot there made her uncomfortable.

She continued, "I walked the labyrinth before, for the first time, when I encountered a health crisis simultaneously with a promotion issue at work. Looking back on it now, I can't believe there was a question in my mind about what needed to be taken care of first. But then, it seemed like I needed some guidance to get to the best answer. I came out of that first walk very clear that I needed to address my health or there wouldn't be a job or a promotion to worry about. But over time, as I healed, I had to face something very scary. I had worked all my life. I never much thought about ideas like toxic work. The health crisis combined with the insights I got through walking the labyrinth were making it clear to me that I was in an untenable position. This one, this last walk, has given me the courage to face the fear and the darkness—really, a terror of being out of work. But the peace that I've gotten to is the potent realization that it's better to let it go. I have to. The health crisis was a wake-up call. Walking the labyrinth has helped me to make peace with a scary proposition—starting over with something else, some other work, someplace else. It has helped me to see both the path and the perfection. One step at a time. One step at a time."

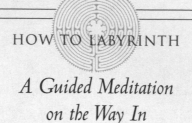

A Guided Meditation
on the Way In

Visualize yourself at the entrance to the labyrinth. You have only one choice to make: whether or not to enter.

After completing your preparations, identifying intention, and tucking the mantra into your mental backpack, take a moment at the entrance—even before you take the first step. Observe the actual path you will walk. In some cases, you will be able to see the entire labyrinth. In others, like the giant meadow labyrinth I got lost in, the entirety will not be visible. Whether or not you can see it, visualize the three-part journey you are about to embark on. Bless the journey, the pilgrim, the path, your fellow travelers, and anything else in the environs.

In this pause before you begin, stand silent and still. Allow yourself to experience the stillness. What does it feel like, this lack of motion? How often do you let yourself stand really still and pay attention?

Out of the stillness will come the movement to carry you forward on this journey. Don't rush this moment. Let it fully envelop you. When the still-ness is complete, the movement will follow, naturally and at its own pace.

As you stand poised at the entrance of the labyrinth, can you connect with the sacred, the holy? Can you offer a prayer before you begin your journey? A blessing, a thanksgiving, or a supplication? Is it your intention that this journey be a pilgrimage? Now is the time to honor that intention, to speak it to yourself, to allow yourself to hear it spoken, and to claim it. Concentrate deeply on whatever intention you will hold for the journey. Then, as you take the first step onto the path, let your mantra begin, like a rhythm, to inform the pace of your walk.

Now, as you begin walking, notice how your body is feeling as it makes the transition from standing still to finding its own pace. Keep asking yourself what you are feeling. Be aware of your *emotional* body as well as your physical body. Ask yourself how your joints and muscles are feeling as they swing into the movement of walking. Ask also what you are feeling in your heart and in your gut. Allow your pace to come from your feelings.

Walk at your own pace and stay in your own experience. As swimming coaches advise, "Swim in your own lane!" This is good advice for labyrinth walking as well. Put all your attention and focus on what you are doing. You need to disregard how others are walking. Neither compare nor care how others are moving. Can you stay so focused on your own walking that you do not pay attention to those around you? Meanwhile, are you respectful of others in their space? Are you comfortable with passing others whose pace is slower than yours? Are you comfortable acknowledging or greeting other people along the way? Do what feels natural for you, and realize it is all right not to acknowledge others on the path.

Step by Step

Go at your own pace and honor whatever that is. Or stop if you want to. Let go of judgment. This is your own experience. Recall the intention that you set for yourself at the outset. Are you still being true to your intention?

Perhaps you are walking to a particular mantra or meditation. Perhaps you are holding a particular question in mind as you walk. As you feel yourself hitting your stride, allow your mind to focus on the words, the syllables, and the sounds of the mantra. Integrate them into your pace.

Maybe you will be able to use your pace as a background rhythm against which you are able to clear your mind completely. You may find that you are entering a deep state of meditation. You are able to hear the voice of your own truth, and be open to divine guidance in whatever way it may come to you. Many meditation traditions have this as the goal. For many, crossing the bridge from everyday thoughts to their own mental sacred space is most effectively done through labyrinth walking. Ask yourself, "Is this true for me? For this walking of the labyrinth?"

You are also bringing your whole body with you in the process. In so doing you are able to experience the meditation kinesthetically, and the rhythm of your walking contributes to the meditative process. Ideally your pace should be effortless, allowing the movement to lull you into meditation as a baby is lulled into sleep by rocking. It may be that you are nowhere near being in a state of meditation, that you still have many things on your mind. If so, fret not. Again, I invite you to pay attention. Notice what you are thinking about, notice what you are distracted by. Is there music? Is it helping to bring you into peacefulness, or is it distracting? What keeps catching your eye as you move round and round? Is there a message in any of this for you?

Bring your full awareness to your walking.

Perhaps you need to make adjustments to your pace. Speed up, slow down, or change your rhythm to better fit how you are feeling now, as opposed to how you felt at the beginning. Do you feel like moving faster and passing those ahead of you? Would you rather be going slower, or do you want to step off the path and rest for moment? Are you staying true to your intention?

Preparation for the Center

As you continue on your journey to the center—your own center, and the center of the labyrinth—you are still in the first phase of a three-part experience. This can be a time to let go of anything that you feel you do not wish to carry with you and to make yourself ready to receive that for which you have come.

There are many ways in which to incorporate the image of letting go into your walk. One is to concentrate on your breathing, allowing each exhale to take with it that which you no longer need. Another is to concentrate on your footsteps and to allow each step to move you further away from that which you no longer want and closer to that which you are now choosing. Use any image that works for you. The main thing is to make yourself ready, and to remember your intention.

Maybe, nearing the center, you do not feel in a meditative state. Or perhaps you find that suddenly you are distracted as you approach the center. Bring your attention back to whatever you are feeling. Remember your mantra. Review your intention. Has your walk carried you closer to your intention? Have you allowed your attention to deepen as you have gone further along the path? Allow your breath to carry you deeper into yourself as you take the last few turns, deeper into the labyrinth.

Questions for the Journey

1. How is my body feeling as it transitions from standing still to finding its own pace?

2. What am I feeling in my heart and in my gut?

3. Am I staying true to my intention?

4. How does it feel now that I have hit my stride?

5. Do I feel safe?

6. Can I let myself go, and really sink into the experience?

7. If not, why not? What is holding me back?

8. How can I use this time on the way in as a preparation for being in the center?

CHAPTER 5

At the Center

For many labyrinth walkers in our goal-oriented culture, the experience of stepping into the center is the whole reason for walking the labyrinth in the first place. To get there. To find the center. To be in the middle.

So what *is* the center? What is it that we want to be in the middle of? "Are we there yet?" we ask, on many levels, like children on a car trip. The idea of the center can bring up many questions. If you asked one thousand people what the center means to them, you probably would get at least one thousand responses. The center is whatever you find there. It is the truth that has been

Elaine Foster in the center.

unlocked for you. For many labyrinth walkers the center represents the Divine. Some place God in the center. Some place Christ in the center. Buddhists may place Buddha in the center. Others see it as a map of the heavenly capital, the city of God. For those who do not subscribe to a religious tradition, the center can hold the essence of truth, the place of connection with one's higher self, the image of that still point within. For some, it represents the realm of Divine Feminine, the life force of the Goddess.

On one level, it is easy to answer where the center is. If the pathway keeps going, you are not there yet. When the path comes to an end, in the middle of the labyrinth, and there is nowhere to go but back out again, you are at the center. Unlike mazes, labyrinths always have clearly defined centers. When you can go no further inward, you are there. This concept—that there is a center—can bring great comfort after the movement of being on the pathway.

Another feature of all labyrinths is that the center is in the middle, not off to one side, so that when you get to the center you are in the very middle of the design. In the case of the many circular labyrinths, when you are in the center you are equidistant from the outer edges of the pattern. This feeling of being in the absolute center holds its own special appeal.

There is a natural reaction that most people seem to have when they reach the center. A silence falls over them. Some people start to worship or quietly say a prayer. Some bow to the north, south, east, and west. Some fall to their knees. Some assume a sitting meditation position. It is as if they have come into the center of the universe, the sacred circle within the sacred circle of life. Many express a sense of awe. This is a time for contemplation—to draw in the impressions of the journey, to meditate on the insights that have come to you, to express gratitude for the day, for life itself, and to begin to think about the trip back out.

Ideally you will have traversed not only the path into the center of the labyrinth, but also the contours of your inner self. The walk to the center of the labyrinth can open your eyes to what you are, who you are, the guidance that resides deep within. What you discover there may have been inside you all the time, but the labyrinth may draw it out.

You also may find yourself feeling a visceral sense of connection to those who have walked the labyrinth in the past: pilgrims in medieval France seeking a stronger relationship to Christ, ancients seeking good fortune or hidden truth. Arriving at the center can be a transformative event. One walker describes being drawn into the center. "I feel as though part of me is connected to this ancient symbol of light and healing. Perhaps wisdom and enlightenment will greet me at the center (of my being)."

People are sometimes caught unaware by their reactions when they arrive at

I love celebrating the centering process. I believe this is a spiritual journey. At the center is the gathering of energies. There is a profound sense of being in a sacred space.
—BOOK OF REFLECTIONS

the center. "Why do I always cry at the center?" one walker asks. She says that she has come to realize the tears are "not tears of pain, but tears of joy." Arriving at the center of the labyrinth fills her with a sense of "knowing I have come home to where I belong."

Why does the center of the labyrinth move people so? I know I learned from my first walk on the labyrinth to always bring along a few "sacred Kleenexes," for the journey. For many people tears seem to be part of the process of walking. It touches something within the heart that has been long encased. This crying seems to wash away the emotional crust we all form.

I have noticed over the years that children seem to be particularly drawn to being not just in the center of the labyrinth but right in the *middle* of the center. They often push each other out of the way so that they can be in the center. I have noticed that many children, if not instructed to follow the pathway, will run right into the center first. I think there is an almost overwhelming curiosity on their part to know what it feels like to be in the center. Perhaps it is like being on the tip-top of a rock or being "King of the Castle."

At the same time, I have noticed that many grown-ups seem to try to avoid being right in the middle. They make their way circumspectly around the edge of the Chartres-type labyrinth centers. In the much smaller centers of the classical labyrinths, they sometimes do not even take that last step forward directly into the middle of the center.

You can learn as much from paying attention to how you behave in the center as from noticing how you move along the path. I learned this early in my labyrinth career when I taught a workshop at Wainwright House in Rye, New York, using their now reconstructed outdoor labyrinth. It was a simple version of the Chartres pattern outlined in white stones and shells, and at that time it had a large tree in the center. I did not like the experience of reaching the center of this labyrinth. I had grown used to the center of a labyrinth being an open space—a space that you filled with your own experience. I liked standing in the center. When I reached the center at Wainwright House, I felt a strong urge to pick up the tree and move it—it was standing in my center. I was surprised how much it bothered me. I walked around the tree. Finally I hugged the tree, but still I resented the tree's presence in the center. I have a similar problem with the seven-circuit stone labyrinth on the grounds of the Omega Institute in Rhinebeck, New York. The builders of this labyrinth put a pile of stones in the center. When I get to the center of a labyrinth, I want to be in the center, right in the middle. Nothing else will do.

The Center at Chartres

I truly felt the world axis here, the world navel.
—Book of Reflections

Is there something innately unique and sacred about being at the center of a labyrinth—a feeling that you can have only there? Some people strongly believe there is. I have long sensed that the centers of all well-used and loved labyrinths, permanent and portable, have high concentrations of "good vibrations"—like the feeling of deep spirituality that some people feel when they worship in a church or synagogue that has been loved and used for many years. Researchers have carefully measured frequencies of the energetic vibrations throughout Chartres Cathedral using a Bovis biometer, which measures site intensity, according to Blanche Merz in her book *Points of Cosmic Energy*. Perhaps not surprisingly, they found the highest vibrations in two locations: at the high altar, and at the center of the labyrinth. Each individual's ability to receive and relate to the energy of the center varies enormously. If being right in the middle of the center does not feel like the right place for you to be, honor that feeling and don't go there.

My most intense experience in the center was in September 1996 when my husband and I traveled to France with Lauren Artress and Robert Ferré to visit the Chartres Cathedral labyrinth. For two evenings, after it was closed to the public, we were literally locked into the cathedral. We were allowed to remove the chairs and walk the labyrinth. I was overwhelmed at the enormity of the experience of being in that beautiful and sacred place, walking the labyrinth and feeling those ancient stones through the thin soles of my ballet slippers. When I got to the center, I stood completely still.

Then I had a spontaneous sensation of a memory from some time past. I am not certain what it was, but I believe it may have been a past-life experience. I do not expect all of you to believe this. If someone had told me a day before it happened that I would have this experience, I would have had a hard time believing it myself. But it was as real to me then as typing these words is to me now, and it remains so to this day. I was aware that I had left my body—my 1996 Helen Curry body—and that I was in an entirely different time and place. I was still in Chartres Cathedral, but I was very high up, on a scaffolding. There were several people around me and I could see stretched out in front of me the back side of one of the enormous stained-glass windows lying face-down flat on a huge frame. Then, as suddenly as I had experienced the memory, I was back in my 1996 body standing on the floor in the center of the labyrinth.

Without a moment's hesitation I felt that I wanted to go back again to where I had just been. And it happened: I was back in the previous scene. I moved forward to get a better look at the back of the window. I could clearly see gobs of lead that held the pieces of stained glass in place. I wanted to touch the thick rough backs of the pieces of colored glass, but someone pushed me away. They wouldn't let me touch the window. I was aware that I was a young boy, and that the others around me were older men. I looked around to get a better idea of where I was, and I noticed that just over my right shoulder far below me on the floor I could see the labyrinth. It was a beautiful design laid in blue-gray stones against the pale brown of the rest of the floor. I could see it in its entirety from where I was standing. I had seen it many times before. I knew just how far down the nave it was from the west entrance, so it helped to orient me within the huge space of the cathedral.

I looked around some more and saw many large ropes and pulleys and I realized that they were getting ready to hoist the window into its place on the wall. I understood that I was an apprentice to the guild that made the scaffolding, and that I needed to get out of the way.

And then it was over. I was back in 1996, standing on the floor in the center of the labyrinth overcome by the beauty, the clarity, and the impact of the experience. I began to cry. Later when I looked up it was right to that window. I knew exactly which one it was. I have been convinced beyond a shadow of a doubt by this experience that the labyrinth was laid into the floor of the cathedral at the time it was rebuilt in A.D. 1201. It was not an afterthought, as some have suggested. I know because I was there.

Never have I experienced anything like this before or since. All I know is that at that moment, circumstances conspired to allow me to turn back the pages to a time when the labyrinth was new. It explains why, when I first walked the labyrinth in 1993, I knew from a place deep within me that I had done it before.

Occurrences such as this are rare but not unheard of. I have talked with people who felt that while walking a labyrinth they traveled back in time and became pilgrims seeking a connection to the Holy Land. Don't let expectations lead you to disappointment. But rejoice if you are so blessed.

Different Labyrinths, Different Centers

Labyrinths with different kinds of centers invite different kinds of meditations. All I have described so far can be applied to any labyrinth walk under any circumstance. What may vary is the length of time available to you. Unless you are walking alone or using a finger labyrinth, you will need to be mindful of

When I got to the center I prayed to God at the fourth petal, then momentarily abandoned God at the sixth and forgot heaven existed. Then gradually came back to God as I approached the path leading out.

—BOOK OF REFLECTIONS

how long you can stay in the center without creating a logjam behind you on the labyrinth. The classical seven-circuit labyrinths usually have small centers, big enough to accommodate only one person at a time. In this type of labyrinth, you may experience the center as a single step and a breath in, then out again—a small acknowledgment on the continuum of the journey.

The Chartres-style labyrinths have relatively large centers that are made up of six petals. Because of this design, the center is often referred to as "the rose." In the Christian tradition the rose is a symbol of Mary and represents the feminine energy of the Divine. For me the feminine energy of the center is distinctly different from the more masculine energy of the pathway.

According to Lauren Artress, Keith Critchlow, and others, the six petals have a further significance in that they stand for the six days of creation. It has been suggested that each petal represents a different realm of creation. I like to spend a few moments in each petal. If it is too crowded for my body to fit

---

LESSONS FROM THE LABYRINTH

"Once I was in what I knew was the ultimate center, I did not want to leave. It was a mystical experience. I felt that I met the foundress of our order of Sisters of Notre Dame who was born in Amiens, France, and who must have known the labyrinth. I met my mother, who assured me she loves heaven and there is constant music there. I met my father still living in minerals. And I answered a very important question about being alone and being in community. It was a prayerful experience."

—BOOK OF REFLECTIONS

in, I try to focus my consciousness there. I say a prayer of gratitude to each one of the petals, and then wait to see if there might be a message for me from any of them. We have few enough opportunities in our lives to honor the various aspects of creation; I enjoy doing it whenever I can. I find that this concept relates well to the Hindu tradition that we all start out as minerals and progress through plants, animals, and humans in our many reincarnations on the way to Nirvana.

As you make your way around the circle of petals, you may feel that you have moved from the realm of matter into the realm of spirit. Sometimes I can feel my connection to the Divine more clearly in the sixth petal than I can right in the middle of the center. It all depends. In my best moments I see the entire center as the place of the Holy of Holies, including all of the realms of creation. I can see the Divine in everything and everyone, including myself.

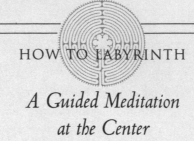

A Guided Meditation
at the Center

There comes a moment in every labyrinth walk when you realize that the center looms ahead of you, and you know that you will make it. It is a few short steps away. Does this realization change your awareness? Do you feel yourself relax just a bit knowing that you will get there? Do you slow your pace to savor those last few steps? Do you speed up like a runner at the finish line? Does it feel like the last few feet of a climb to the top of Mt. Everest?

Do you feel a sense of completion, of a job well done, or that it is time for a well-earned rest? Or perhaps you feel a sense of loss because something is coming to an end, and things are going to be different. You know that, for the time being at least, this will be the end of the forward movement. The time of preparation is over, and this is the moment you have been waiting for. Yet you may not feel ready.

So often in our lives do we work for something, anticipate it, move toward it, wait for it, only to find when the time comes we cannot be present. Or we are disappointed, and think that it should have been different. For some, arriving at the center can be a letdown. If this is so for you, I invite you to let go of any judgment. Sit with the feeling. Your perceptions may change over time. There is nothing wrong with you if bells and whistles don't go off every time you get to the center. It may seem as though nothing has happened—until much later, when you realize that a subtle shift, a new awareness, has occurred.

Depending on the circumstances of the walk, you may have to wait to enter the center until others have moved out of the way. How do you feel about this? Are you bothered by having your pace or your thoughts interrupted? Are you impatient at having to wait your turn? Are you angry at the others for being where you want to be?

Can you see the perfection in your situation as you wait to enter the center? When the pilgrim is ready, the center will appear, and the way will be clear.

Notice carefully how you enter the center. Are you reticent to take the last step? Are you humbled by even the thought of being there? Do you stride in with confidence?

Let your way of entering the center—your pace, your attitude, your body language—be your statement to yourself, and to the universe, about who you choose to be in this moment. Feel the power of that statement; walk into it and let it envelop you.

What does it feel like to step into the center? What line have you crossed in your consciousness, and on your journey? How is the energy of the center different from that of the pathway?

If you find yourself hesitating, you might ask yourself whether you are afraid of the center, of being exactly in the middle? Does it hold more power for you than the edges of the center? Do you feel you do not deserve to be there? Do you shy away from being the center of attention? Do you secretly want to be there? Would you do it if you were all alone?

The Six-Petal Center

In the large center of the Chartres-style labyrinth, you may want to step into each petal to acknowledge each realm of creation. Remember that the realms go clockwise from the bottom left, and they go from the most corporeal to the most ethereal.

Beginning to the left as you enter the center, the first petal represents the mineral kingdom, and our Mother Earth. I pause to give thanks to the Earth and ask for her healing in all the many ways that we know she needs it. What of the mineral kingdom presents itself to you for attention? Rocks? Stones? Boulders? Mountains? The whole Earth itself?

Next to the left, at the 9:00 position, is the plant kingdom. I give thanks to all of the vegetation that grows on this beautiful green planet, without which we could not sustain life. In your walk, do any particular plants come to mind as being of special importance at this time?

Up at 11:00 is the animal kingdom. I send my gratitude and my blessings to all creatures great and small. What about the animals in your life that you wish to bless?

At 1:00 is the human kingdom and I give thanks for people in all of their wondrous diversity. Can you feel specific members of the human community calling for your prayers and concentration?

At 3:00 is the place of the angelic kingdom. There I acknowledge the amazing resources available to all of us in our special guides and angels. I have the best possible team of them, with whom I am in daily contact, from the parking place angels to totem animals to spirit guides. I couldn't do it without them. What about you? What comes to your mind to bless and acknowledge at this petal?

Finally, the last petal is the realm of the unknown, or the place of the Divine. What connection do you feel here? Is it different from being in the center of the center?

Being in the Center

Even in a large group each person should take time to stand still in the center for few moments. I suggest that you remain still for at least one full breath, inhalation and exhalation. If you are skilled at meditating and can clear your mind completely, do not move until the next thought comes in.

In labyrinths with small centers, the time in the center can be like another step along the path, part of the continuum of the total experience. I liken this to a glimpse of enlightenment. For most of us transformation happens in a flash. Enlightenment is a split-second realization that may change your life forever. It is not usually an event that lasts for several minutes. It may take several minutes or a whole lifetime to grasp it, but the actual moment of transformation is almost instantaneous.

I love using this image when walking these kinds of labyrinths, and I never feel that I have been cheated out of a long, luxurious time in the center. Neither experience is better than the other. They are just different.

No matter where you are in the center, be still. Out of the stillness will come the movement to carry you forward into the third phase of this labyrinth journey: from the center back out to the entrance. When the stillness is complete, the movement will follow.

Does the stillness of the center have a different quality from the stillness of the entrance? For me it does not usually contain the same feelings of anticipation. Often I actually experience a mild sense of reluctance within the stillness of the center, knowing that I must leave this special place and begin moving back out toward the "real" world again.

As you prepare to leave the center, give thanks for what you have received thus far. Review the intention that you set for yourself at the beginning. Are you still remaining true to your intention?

Remember the mantra or meditation that you used along the way. Let your intention be your guide and the mantra inform your pace as you step out of the center and begin your journey back to the beginning. Ask yourself what, if anything, has come up for you at the center.

Questions for the Journey

1. How does it feel when you realize that you have made it to the center?

2. What does it feel like to step into the center?

3. What line have you crossed in your consciousness, and on your journey?

4. What does the center mean to you?

5. Are you comfortable being right in the middle?

6. How is the energy of the center different from that of the pathway?

7. Are you still being true to your intention?

8. What about your mantra or meditation? Is it also informing your time at the center?

9. Has anything special come to your attention at the center?

10. How is the stillness at the center different from the stillness at the start?

CHAPTER 6

On the Way Out

Where there is hatred, let me sow love . . .
—PRAYER OF ST. FRANCIS

When you reach the center—perhaps dropping into a sitting meditation position, or kneeling to offer a prayer of thanks—you have reached a different and special place. It may be hard for you to leave.

But there is good reason to go back. For many people, the journey back from the labyrinth's center is the most fruitful part of the walk. It is a time for reflection. Now is the time to try to absorb the insights that have come to you in the course of the walk. On this stage of the walk, new perspectives you have gained can sink in, become part of you. This period of time is a gift. How

*Kids in center
with ball.*

many other occasions in our lives do we have time not only to reach an insight, but to "own" it as well? What a welcome departure from the crazy norm of daily life in which we are constantly telling ourselves to get on to the next thing. One of the unique characteristics of the labyrinth meditation is that the journey back from the center is as long as the journey to the center. The outward-bound half of the trip is a mirror image of the inward-bound half.

Integrating the Experience

For many people, the path out becomes an opportunity to think about the practical questions of how to integrate into their daily lives the insights they have gained on their walk. "Do I need to make changes?" "What is going to be involved?" "What are the implications going to be for me and for others in my life?" "Where should I begin?" "How can I make the most of what I have learned?" "How can I keep this feeling alive?" "What's the next step?"

You might concentrate on the walk itself, asking how this experience compares to what you felt at the beginning, on the walk in, or at the center. "How have I changed?" you might ask. Your thoughts might focus on a specific issue in your life—a relationship, a problem in your job or career, a health concern—or it might turn to larger questions, such as your relationship to the world or to the sacred. Your reflection might lead to a deeper meditation. For some, the path out helps bring the sacred into everyday life. The walk back engages you in the potential for transformation. "How can I take this back out into the world?" "How can it make a difference in my life and in the lives of others?"

Sometimes, you get a surprising new insight on the path out. Something that you were previously unaware of—something you overlooked—springs forth suddenly. Having been on the labyrinth for a considerable time—perhaps one-half hour or more—some reach a special place of simultaneous relaxation and heightened awareness. The turns and counterturns on the path out deepen the meditative state. Insights often come more easily. Like pockets of air that have been trapped beneath the surface, or streams of bubbles in a glass of champagne, ideas rush up to the surface from some place within. The walker has truly become a pilgrim ready for the lesson.

Like all homeward trips, the return from the center of the labyrinth can be an emotional experience. Walking, breathing, and thinking have slipped into a rhythm. The distractions of daily life have been banished at least for the duration of the walk. You feel attentive and attuned to the sights and sounds around you. You feel spiritually centered. You may feel a heightened sense of peace and well-being.

Other people find it hard to contain themselves on the journey home. They

I am always reluctant to finish a journey and return home. Yet I'm always joyful at the prospect of being again in my nest after the journey. And so I reluctantly end this journey and joyfully return home.

—BOOK OF REFLECTIONS

can't wait to share their thoughts with friends and family. For others, the trip back is simply a time to savor. Some people—children particularly—can hardly hold back their joy (and why should they?). I have seen people skip and dance on their way out of the labyrinth—sometimes, dancing with each other.

It's important to "walk with intention" through to the end of the labyrinth walk. Otherwise, you miss the full impact of the experience. You cheat yourself out of something worthwhile. Unfortunately, not everyone sees the value of this part of the labyrinth experience. Like others in our goals-obsessed society, they pour all their energy into getting to the "goal" of the center of the labyrinth. After reaching the center, they tune out. Some people, after walking slowly and mindfully to the center of the labyrinth, turn heels and rush-rush-rush back out as fast as they can. In their mind, they're already back in the car and off to their next activity. During my first labyrinth workshop, Lauren Artress shared the story of one such woman.

The woman started the walk and seemed to immerse herself in the experience, winding carefully back and forth along the labyrinth's path until she reached the center. But after several minutes in the center—clearly the "goal" and the climax of the labyrinth walk, in her mind—she got up and simply walked across the canvas, making a beeline across the paths and walls of the labyrinth until she reached the edge, and sat down.

She soon noticed that the other walkers didn't follow her course. After reaching the center, they got back on the path of the labyrinth and wound their way back out to the entrance. Then it dawned on the woman. She had not completed the walk. She realized that she had only done half of it. And she saw the same pattern in her life. She was great at starting things, but she often didn't finish them. Her home was filled with half-finished projects.

She walked straight to the center and started the "return trip" of her labyrinth walk all over again. This time, she followed the path of the labyrinth until she returned to the beginning.

Not only did she learn something about herself, she also used the labyrinth to begin a deep and important change in the way she lived her life. This is an excellent example of how the labyrinth can promote psychological growth. Some people have even told me that a labyrinth walk has taught them as much as months of therapy. One teenaged boy said he learned so much from labyrinth walking, he didn't think he needed to go to college! I would never suggest that the labyrinth is a substitute for therapy, psychological counseling, a doctor's advice, or a college education. However, I do think it can be used as a complement to any of these. People have said that they have undertaken regular labyrinth walks as added support during twelve-step programs and found that it was a wonderful adjunct to the recovery process. It's a way to go deeper into the experience and bring "inner knowledge" to the complicated problem of addiction, or to any other healing process you may be undertaking.

There are many other lessons that can be gained as well on the way back, if you pay attention. I can attest to this. After years of labyrinth walking, I'm still learning. I've learned, for example, how important it is to simply *slow down.* I tend to do the labyrinth at full speed. I often move quite quickly on my way into the center. I suppose that I'm impatient to get there. After a while, I start slowing down. By the time I begin the journey back, I am moving carefully and deliberately. I am walking with a sense of reverence. Arriving in the center usually slows me down. On the homeward trip, I start to want to stretch the journey out, to make it last longer. I have noticed that I never rush out the way I rush in.

Accepting the Lessons

The labyrinth can hold up a mirror to our lives. A mother of two young children said that, although she didn't know what a labyrinth was, when she heard about an open house at a local retreat center in which walking a labyrinth was

Lessons from the Labyrinth

> *"Having never heard of walking the labyrinth, I had no preconceived notions. However, having only experienced solitary meditation, I was under the impression that this experience would be similar. I learned different. First, I felt heavy and confused. There were so many people in my 'space' it made me feel very vulnerable. Then people started coming at me, and it frustrated me. I wanted everyone to 'go away' and let me do this by myself. Then I got to the center and sat down. Sitting there, in a more typical meditation posture, I refocused, relaxed, and began to feel rejuvenated. My experience on the way out was light and joyful. Instead of being angry at the people around me for 'getting in my way,' I felt love and blessed everyone I passed. Alleluia!"*
>
> —*Book of Reflections*

one of the activities, she was determined to go. She didn't know what to expect, and when the day came for the family outing, it was raining.

"We arrived," she says, "saw a grove of trees, and, thinking it was hedge walls, thought that was our destination. (I was also hopeful that the trees would offer some protection from the rain.)"

What they found, instead of the protection of hedges, was a path of stones set into the top of a rise. "It seemed so—well—flat," she says. But with no preparation or explanation of any kind, with two young children and "a slightly skeptical spouse," she started to walk—getting soaked in the process by the rain.

"My husband spent time in contemplation in the center," she says. "He shed his skepticism on the path out. My nine-year-old daughter walked in mindful nine-year-old fashion the entire path in and out. My six-year-old son, crazy about mazes and puzzles, ran the path all the way in to get to the center first. As he started on the path back out, he lost interest. He ran to the outside, then back in along no particular path to try and hurry his parents along on our meditative pace.

"I felt a desperation (and resignation) at trying to rein in the six-year-old-boy energy so that he might not disturb the other few walkers in the rain. And yet despite the distractions, I found it compelling. It felt like a perfect reflection of my state—right in the middle of the river of life, the kids, the rain, distractions, and yet still we try and touch some semblance of a more contemplative energy."

The labyrinth can offer you a sense of reassurance that, despite the problems that you face in your life, life is all right. Life is good.

Sometimes the guidance we receive by the time we leave the labyrinth is not what we started out looking for. A young man once walked the labyrinth in the hope of achieving resolution about an important decision he had to make. He wanted to know whether to make a marriage proposal. The idea was particularly dear to him because he had come from a large and fairly happy family. In contrast, the woman he was considering marrying seemed lukewarm at best about the prospect of children. So he walked the labyrinth with a very clear intention of seeking guidance in the same way people write to advice columnists. He hoped for something sharply delineated—some answer like, "Ask her," or "Don't."

He didn't get exactly that answer. At the end of the walk, the questions he started with—Are we right for each other? If I insist on children, will it lead to something beautiful or to the wrong path for all involved? Will we simply become another chilling statistic in the divorce rate?—were still there. But he had a newfound sense that all would be well. Something coalesced in his brain—maybe in his heart as well. Despite a tangle of thoughts about risk and love, he began to realize that even with the best of intentions there are no guarantees.

This young man discovered for himself a mystery of the labyrinth: it turns us back to our own inner knowledge.

The Last Step Out

I always turn around to face the entrance upon taking the last step out of the labyrinth. I do it so that I can have a moment of prayer before going back out into the world. For me this feels most comfortable to do while I am facing the labyrinth with my back to the world, so to speak. But there is no reason it cannot be done while facing the world with one's back to the labyrinth.

The point of the prayer is to have a moment to express my gratitude, to acknowledge the Divine with awe and reverence, and to honor my labyrinth walk as having been a sacred experience. Many people have a similar ritual when they reach the end. This may not be comfortable or necessary for you. As with other parts of the walk, follow your own guidance.

Regardless of what you do, it is important to be respectful of those who pause in prayer at the entrance and give them a moment before rushing past them on the way in. This would seem to be a common courtesy, but I have been tapped on the shoulder during such a moment, as I stood still with my eyes closed, obviously in prayer at the entrance.

Acknowledging the stillness at the end of the walk and stepping into it concentrates the energy of the walk. Similarly, the closing prayer grounds the walk. These small practices help keep the afterglow from dissipating as one moves back into day-to-day life. The different kinds of stillness are as important as the times of movement. Yin and yang. Masculine and feminine. Body and mind. A large part of the labyrinth's healing power comes from its ability to bridge the gaps between opposites. Through the labyrinth, the opposites come together in union and unity. The path out symbolizes this sense of the meeting of opposites and gives us a symbol to bring back into the world. The ending is the beginning.

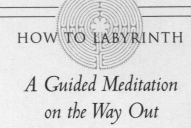

A Guided Meditation
on the Way Out

Just as there is a moment in every labyrinth walk when you have made it to the center, so too there is a moment in every labyrinth walk when you know you must leave the center. In this moment it becomes clear that the time is right to get moving again, to resume the journey, and to begin to make your way back out of the labyrinth. Only you will know when that time has come. Listen to your inner voice on this and respect it.

Before you resume your journey I invite you to take a moment to honor the stillness. Notice the nature of that stillness. Does it feel different from the way the stillness felt at the start of your labyrinth walk? Are you excited to be leaving or are you experiencing some reluctance?

When you are ready to begin moving, do so with intention. This is a good time to restate your intention to yourself and, if it feels comfortable, to begin saying your mantra again. Most of all, pay attention to how it feels to begin the movement. Notice how it might be different from the way the

movement began at the start of your walk. Ask yourself if getting to the center and spending time there, even if it was for just a moment, has made a difference in how you are starting to walk back out.

As you begin to make your way out of the center and move along the pathway, notice the pace of your movement. Is it different from the way you were moving on the way in? Or, is it just about the same? As you begin to gain your rhythm, remember to walk at your own pace, to honor the speed that your body wants to be moving. Do not be bothered by the way others are moving around you on the pathways. Stay in your own experience and do not force yourself to do it the same way you did it on the way in. It may feel very different now than it did then, and this is the time to honor that.

Are you walking to the rhythm of your mantra or meditation? Are you going slower than on the walk in? Are you speeding up? Consider the earlier parts of your walk. Consider your time in the center. As you follow the path out of the center notice that it is exactly the same path that you took on the way in, only you are now going in the opposite direction. How does this feel and look? Are you seeing things differently than you did on the way in? Take time to notice how your perspective may have changed the way you see things.

Pay attention to these differences and see if they help to inform you about how you live your life. Is there a message here for you? If so, what is it? Do not be concerned if these things are not clear to you at this point. Remember that you are still in the midst of the experience, but it is worth paying attention to all of this and seeing how it informs your thoughts after you have finished your walk.

As you make your way back along the path, are you able to clear your mind and stay in your rhythm? Are you repeating your mantra and achieving a natural state of meditation as you walk? Again, this may be easier or harder for you to do than it was on the way in. Notice the differences in this as well.

As always, you need not be judgmental about any of this. Don't think that you are doing it wrong if you were able to meditate on the way in and now find that you cannot meditate on the way out. Or, perhaps you are able to meditate now, whereas you didn't on the way in. Remember, there is no wrong way to do a labyrinth walk.

Leaving the Labyrinth

Eventually you will come to the inevitable moment of returning to the entrance. You will see that it is just ahead of you and you will know that you are coming to the end of your labyrinth walk. You are back at the beginning. In a labyrinth, it is a simple and fundamental truth that the beginning really is the end, and that the end really is the beginning.

How does it feel to be taking those last few steps on the path before stepping back out into the world? Do you want to rush right out and get on with your life, or do you want to linger and make the journey last for as long as possible?

Like the moment of realizing that you have made it to the center, the moment of realizing that you have made it to the end can cause a shift in your perceptions. Notice if this is so for you. Ask yourself how you are feeling and whether or not you have stayed true to your original intention.

Just as there is no correct way to enter the

labyrinth or enter the center, so too is there no correct way to leave it. Still, pay attention to how you choose to depart. Notice if you are walking out in reverence, slowing down to make it last, speeding up to get it over with, or striding out in confidence. Again, there may be a lesson for you.

I invite you to take a moment to notice the stillness at the end of the walk. Can you feel a difference from the stillness at the beginning, or at the center? What can you take from the stillness? Does some prayer, blessing, or acknowledgment seem fitting as an ending?

Questions for the Journey Out

1. How does it feel to resume the movement?

2. Are you still staying true to your intention?

3. Are you still using your mantra or meditation phrase?

4. Do things seem different to you than they did on the way in?

5. Has the pace of your movement changed?

6. Is it easier or harder now to meditate than it was on the way in?

7. How does it feel to take the last few steps out of the labyrinth?

8. How are the stillness of the entrance, the stillness of the center, and the stillness at the end different from each other?

9. Do you wish to have a final moment of prayer?

CHAPTER 7

After the Walk

I look back and have the strongest sense of just having had an "interlude" with God—intimate,
loving, whole mind, body, spirit. Then to leave feeling sated and renewed—until the next time.
—BOOK OF REFLECTIONS

What do you do after you've left the labyrinth? You easily might think that the walk is over. But if you have received guidance on the intention with which you started your walk, you will want to bring this new wisdom into your life. You won't want to let it drift away.

Tools for Remembrance

I often suggest at labyrinth walks and workshops that journaling materials be made available so that walkers can record their impressions immediately upon finishing the walk, while the experience is still fresh. Some people find that other artistic media serve them better. They draw, paint, or use sculpting materials to capture their impressions of the walk. Offering pens and pencils, markers, crayons, notebooks, a variety of papers, even scissors and glue can give walkers the opportunity to reflect on the walk and express their insights.

Some people bring their own writing journals. The *Book of Reflections*, from which I've been quoting, is a public journal. We've been keeping it for a long time, so that people can share their thoughts and see the thoughts of their fellow travelers. Knowing what others experience on the labyrinth is an invaluable resource for all of us. The book also is a wonderful testimony to creativity. And not just in words: Many people choose to illustrate their comments with symbols that have special meaning to them, or that came up during their walk—suns, mandalas, trees of life. While some of the symbols and anecdotes seem to tap a universal chord, coming up again and again, others are unique.

Many people find that the labyrinth walk offers a rich opportunity for reflection. I invite you to create your own personal "Book of Reflections," a special journal or notebook just for your labyrinth meditations and reflections. A few people carry a small notebook with them on the path. Others wait until the end.

"This is the *last time* I walk the labyrinth without having my own notebook and pen with me! How can I be so silly as to have six months of walking without allowing myself to record the experience for myself?" comments one walker in the *Book of Reflections*. He went on to admit that this was "a minor irritation"—he was also feeling "a flood of joy" in a newfound recognition that the labyrinth is like a mirror of life.

Sharing the Experience

Sharing our stories is also one of the very best ways to make a connection with each other. Connecting with others is one of the deepest and most basic needs of human beings. Over the years, hundreds of people have shared their labyrinth stories with me—in person, over the phone, in notes and letters following their walks. Some have sent me poetry and visual art that they created in the days or weeks after the walk, as they continued to process their experience.

During workshops, I include an opportunity for participants to share with the group their experiences of walking the labyrinth. This storytelling can bring the labyrinth to life in a new way. Most people like to compare others' experiences with their own. It's reassuring to hear that others may have felt uncertain as they began, that others were confused when they came face-to-face with a walker coming out while they were going in, that others had self-doubts. It's empowering to hear that others had positive experiences you had—a strange sense of calm, perhaps an impression that all is well in the world, maybe a special sense of heart connection to someone important to you. And it's also enlightening to hear how others' experiences were vastly different from your own.

Emotional Reactions

"Today is my fiftieth birthday," one walker wrote in the *Book of Reflections*. "I feel both young and old at the same time. Old because I feel the cord that links me to the past—to my mother, her mother, and her mother's mother. Young because I feel that I am able to perceive—and let go! I understood something during my labyrinth walk today, something that has prevented my mother and me from giving and receiving love. I can let that wounded child be loved."

Labyrinth walks can produce unexpected, deeply emotional responses. My own first labyrinth experience is also an example of this. I cried for almost four hours straight during the second day of that retreat. Some might say that that was a bad experience. For me it was wonderful. I loved it. Why? I recognized that the walk was touching a deep emotional chord within me. A gate had been opened. The tears were cleansing. They brought a welcome relief. They were part of a sense of profound homecoming.

It's not unusual for feelings of woundedness to come up during a labyrinth walk. The first reaction may be to recoil from the feelings. However, many experts suggest that such experiences are healing. Reopening these feelings, and looking at them anew, is better than pretending they don't exist. The labyrinth offers a safe haven to examine old wounds, to feel the pain that has been inflicted, and, more often than not, to take the first steps toward healing. As far as those who have had "bad" experiences are concerned, it is important to remember that "bad" is a judgment. Often it is necessary to be made to feel uncomfortable, to be embarrassed, or even to experience pain in order to learn something. "Tonight my Self embraced a very frightened, very young sexually and physically abused child," one man wrote. "I, with the help/nurturing of my higher Self, relived and relieved some of the 40-year-old pain. Thank you, God."

Many people might say this labyrinth walk was a bad experience, dredging up feelings that were better left alone. This walker experienced it as the beginning of what would become a very powerful healing. He called to thank me the next day. It is quite possible to have unpleasant things happen which in the long run, or even immediately, can be very good for growth. The labyrinth walk can often bring up not only the wound, but also the means to heal that wound, to find a way to love the self and others, despite the scar tissue from past traumas.

A woman who came to one of our early walks had lost her husband a few months before. I met her a couple of weeks later and she told me that as a result of walking the labyrinth, she had finally been able to stop crying all the time and had begun the process of moving past her grief.

For those who have lost a loved one, the labyrinth walk quiets the heart to hear and gain access to emotions that may come up. This opening of the heart has helped people process their grief, acknowledge and affirm their feelings, strengthen their memories of the person they have lost, and bring meaning and strength to the move forward.

The Walk Over Time

For those who feel they didn't experience anything, it is possible that they didn't experience anything *yet*. Sometimes it can take a while for us to completely process an experience, and we often don't feel the full impact of it right away. Some people have said that their labyrinth walk seemed to have started before they ever arrived at the event and seemed to go on long afterward as well.

I can think of all kinds of times when the real meaning or significance of something didn't hit until well after the fact. My advice in this case is to just sit with it and see what happens. Realize that the labyrinth works in mysterious ways, and usually in its own time.

What do you choose to bring back to the world after your walk? Remember, no matter what comes up, it is always your choice to take it further. It is likely that bringing the lesson out into the world from the labyrinth will call forth your continued attention and intention. The lessons of the labyrinth can be huge. They can also be small and seemingly insignificant. You might even think that you experienced nothing at all. What is important just after the walk is to actively reflect on all parts of the experience, recording what you recall from each part. Even if you think "nothing" happened, there may be some deep and as yet invisible force at work.

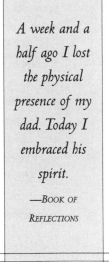

A week and a half ago I lost the physical presence of my dad. Today I embraced his spirit.

—BOOK OF
REFLECTIONS

A Guided Meditation
for Integrating the Walk

Now that you have stepped off the labyrinth, it is time to return your thoughts to all the preparations that you made at the beginning, to gauge the changes you have experienced, to acknowledge where you've been and reflect on where you are going.

Take a few moments to observe how you are feeling—your physical body, your mind, your emotions, your spirit. Think back, or look back at the notes that you made at the beginning of the walk. Look at where you started. Consider where you are, now that you have completed the walk. Is it different? Have you experienced change in one or more of these areas? Actively reflect on the changes.

Consider your attention: Were you able to experience mindfulness on most of the trip? Were you present each step of the way? Did your mind drift off? Did you experience the power of paying attention? Did your attention seem more focused at one part of the walk? Is there anything that comes to mind to which you can attribute your

varying levels of attention? Accept and acknowledge whatever came up for you on this particular journey, including the fading and intensifying of your attention.

Were you able to avoid expectations? Did you receive the guidance you hoped for? Did something completely surprising come up for you? Did you think of yourself as a pilgrim, and did that inform your journey?

What about your meditation or mantra? Did it provide a song for you to dance to? Did you forget it at a certain point, only to come back to it at another time? Was it helpful to you in achieving a meditative state? Or did you find it got in the way?

Did you feel you were able to enter the stillness in different ways and at different points along the walk? Were you able to hear the still, small voice within? What did it say to you?

Now that you have reviewed how every part of you is feeling, what connections do you find with your intention at the beginning of the walk? Are your feelings and intentions connected? Did your intention and pace inform your walk? Did the lessons appear out of paying attention, or did they come when your attention had drifted away from your intention?

Were you seeking a change on your journey? If consciously seeking change is one reason to walk a labyrinth, then consider whether or not you have been pointed in the direction of the change that you clarified at the beginning. Were you sent in a completely different direction?

Bringing What You've Gained Back into the World

After the preparation and the intense contemplation during the three-part walk itself comes the action of bringing forth.

From your state of walking meditation, from experiencing the thought and the word, what action are you now compelled to take to make the lessons concrete in the world? Can you bring your intention to life in thought, word, and deed? What work are you directed to? It may be a personal action. It may be inner work. Maybe you are called to

review how you deal with a particular relationship. It may be something larger.

Questions for the Journey

1. How was the journey?

2. What happened?

3. Did the journey itself and discoveries along the way make a difference in your life?

4. How can your realizations make a difference in the lives of others or in the world?

5. What did you learn about your intention?

6. What did you "see" about yourself that came as a surprise?

7. What do you understand differently now—about yourself and how you live your life?

8. What actions will you take?

PART THREE

THE ADVANCED
LABYRINTH

CHAPTER 8

The Art of Finger Labyrinths

I want to do this every day of my life.
—BOOK OF REFLECTIONS

Wouldn't it be great to be able to take a "labyrinth break" instead of a coffee break at work? It probably would increase your productivity. Think how different airports would be if frazzled travelers had a labyrinth to walk instead of having to park themselves in front of a television set or spend time and money in souvenir shops. Instead of being bored, frustrated, or angry, you could start your trip calm and centered.

It can be done. This is what I call the "no excuses" section of the book. I will show you how to bring the labyrinth into your life no matter where you are. It's easier and easier to find fingerwalking boards with patterns of differ-ent kinds of labyrinths. Various people, some of them colleagues of mine in the Labyrinth Society, create wooden tabletop labyrinths with both classical seven-circuit and Chartres Cathedral patterns. On most, the paths have been carved into the labyrinth, so that there are grooved indentations for the finger to trace. Some boards have left-handed and right-handed labyrinths side by side (see page 105 for an explanation of left-handed and right-handed). The Recommended Resources section of this book has more information on how to locate and acquire these labyrinths.

I will teach you how to make your own "personal" labyrinth to take with you wherever you go and use wherever you happen to be. And I will describe how people have incorporated these portable labyrinths into their day-to-day lives.

You don't have to have walked a full-size labyrinth to get the benefits of a labyrinth meditation. Tracing a labyrinth with a finger or pen can produce many of the same effects. Just like regular labyrinth walks, finger walking can be a daily practice for anyone.

I usually have finger-walking labyrinth boards at public walks of the Labyrinth Project of Connecticut. Sometimes I use these boards as teaching tools to introduce the labyrinth to groups before they walk a full-size labyrinth. Many people will do a finger walk before or after walking the full-size labyrinth. The finger labyrinths have proven to be especially valuable when families bring children to walks. Often parents and children will trace the fin-ger labyrinths together.

There's something relaxing about tracing the lines of the labyrinth. Like counting rosary beads or meditating in the midst of a busy day, it can trans-port us to a different place. An acquaintance of mine traces the lines of a primitive labyrinth pattern on the large, brass knobs of his kitchen cabinets every morning while he waits for his coffee to brew. He finds it centers him before he starts the day. He didn't set out to do this when he bought the knobs; he just liked the way they looked. They had a certain timeless quality that seemed to him a nice counterbalance to his hectic life. Once they were up, he found he was drawn to tracing the path—either with his finger or eyes—whenever he opened the cabinet.

Drawing a Labyrinth: Getting Started

You can find labyrinths on an astonishing array of objects today. It's a sign of the growing interest in them. I've seen labyrinths on all kinds of jewelry, wall hangings, T-shirts, coasters, and box lids. But you don't have to buy a labyrinth to have one in your home. You can create a labyrinth with as little as a pencil and paper. Drawing a labyrinth is not only a way to create a labyrinth but also a relaxing exercise in and of itself.

"I have found that drawing labyrinths is almost addictive," says one of the editors of this book. "There is something so satisfying about it, like connecting the dots in children's games. There's almost a magical aspect to it. Drawing labyrinths is the most immediate and accessible way to introduce labyrinths."

Before getting started, let's review the vocabulary associated with labyrinths. The space where you enter is the "mouth" or "entrance." In most labyrinths, you walk on the "path." The lines you walk between are the "walls."

If the path leads immediately to the left when you enter, it is a "left-handed" labyrinth. If the path leads to the right, it is a "right-handed" labyrinth. As you follow the path, you move toward the "center" of the labyrinth.

Labyrinths are described by how many "circuits" they have. The classical seven-circuit labyrinth has seven "circuits" of paths counting from the outside toward the center. If you number the paths in a classical seven-circuit labyrinth

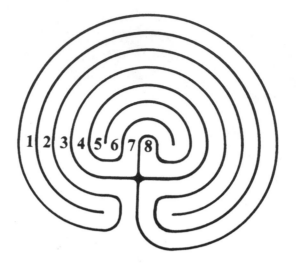

from the outer circuit to the inner circuit, you'll notice that you don't travel in numerical order. Instead, you travel in this order: 3-2-1-4-7-6-5-8 (with "8" as the center).

Sig Lonegren, one of the pioneers of the labyrinth movement, taught me the basic concepts for drawing labyrinths. These are thoroughly explained in a book he wrote, *Labyrinths: Ancient Myths and Modern Uses*, now out of print. Sig also maintains a wealth of information on labyrinths at his Web site (see Recommended Resources on page 249).

A terrific idea for those who don't think they're "artistic" enough to draw their own finger labyrinth is to do a tracing or rubbing of one. People do rubbings of grave markers or antique grillwork, so why not labyrinths?

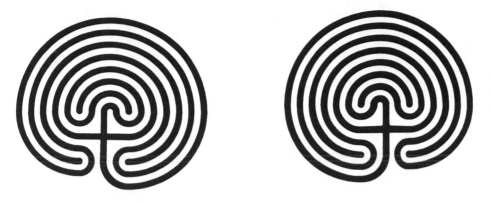

Left- and right-handed labyrinths.

Drawing a Classical Left-Handed, Three-Circuit Labyrinth

We're going to start with a basic "seed pattern" to draw the classical three-circuit labyrinth, the easiest to create.

To draw a three-circuit labyrinth, first draw two lines of equal length—one vertical, one horizontal—that intersect at their midpoints. You should position these crossed lines toward the lower middle of the page; these labyrinths tend to grow larger out of the top than the bottom.

The cross you have drawn contains the four quadrants of the labyrinth. Imagine now that you are going to create a square box that this cross would fit into. Draw dots at the four points where the corners of the box would be. You now have the basic seed pattern for the three-circuit labyrinth.

Now draw your labyrinth. Starting at the top of the vertical line of the cross, take your pencil and draw an arc going clockwise to the first dot to the right—that is, the dot in the corner of the upper right-hand quadrant. You've now created the center for your labyrinth!

Next, move your pencil to the dot at the corner of the upper left-hand quadrant. Trace your pencil in a clockwise pattern in an arc roughly parallel to your first arc, from the dot in the upper left-hand quadrant to the tip of the right end of the horizontal axis of your cross. The line you have drawn is roughly half of a circle.

Now, go to the left end of the horizontal line. Extend the line far enough horizontally to create the width of one pathway. Draw a curving line clockwise from the left end of the horizontal line in an arc, parallel to the lines you previously drew, and connect it to the dot in the lower right-hand quadrant.

Now it's time to draw your last line. Bring your pencil to the dot in the lower left-hand quadrant. Draw a circle clockwise from the dot in the lower left-hand quadrant roughly parallel to your previous lines all the way around the labyrinth to the bottom tip of the vertical line. This line is the outer wall of your labyrinth.

You should now have a classical three-circuit labyrinth. The path begins at the mouth, just to the left of the bottom of the labyrinth, and leads to the left. The labyrinth should look roughly like the one depicted here. If it does, congratulations! You've just drawn your first labyrinth.

Whether or not you are satisfied with the labyrinth that you have drawn, go back to the beginning and draw a new labyrinth, and perhaps repeat the exercise three or four more times. If you keep a journal, you may want to practice drawing the labyrinth there. The more you draw labyrinths, the better you'll get. You'll become more comfortable with the process. Before long, you will know how to draw this labyrinth from memory. Then you will be able to "build" a labyrinth no matter where you are. You've created a portable labyrinth kit that you can walk whenever and wherever you are. Be sure and leave plenty of space between the lines for your path so that you can walk comfortably with your fingers. Here is an extra seed pattern to complete:

Drawing a Classical Right-Handed, Three-Circuit Labyrinth

Why draw a right-handed labyrinth? Drawing a right-handed labyrinth is a challenge for many people. The movement of a right-handed labyrinth is counterclockwise—a direction that we tend to move in less often. But the fact that it forces us to take "the less-taken path" is beneficial. It's good to break the usual pattern, to look at things in a new way. Most significant, knowing how to draw both left- and right-handed labyrinths means that you can make them and walk them in pairs—very effective for right- and left-brain balancing.

Start by following the same steps you used in drawing the left-handed labyrinth. Draw two lines of equal length—one vertical, the other horizontal—that intersect at their midpoints. Then draw the four dots in the outer corners of the four quadrants formed by the horizontal and vertical lines.

Next, move your pencil to the top of the vertical line. Draw an arcing line from the top of the vertical line to the dot in the upper left-hand quadrant, which is the first dot to your left. (Here, things begin to differ from the left-handed labyrinth: You're moving counterclockwise, instead of clockwise.) You've made your labyrinth's center.

Now pick up your pencil and go to the dot in the upper right-hand quadrant. Draw a long, curving arc counterclockwise from the dot in the upper right-hand quadrant, to the left end of the horizontal line, keeping it parallel to your first line.

Next, pick up your pencil and go to the right end of the horizontal line. Draw a long, arcing line counterclockwise, parallel to your first two lines, from the right end of the horizontal line to the dot in the lower left-hand quadrant.

Now, go to the dot in the lower right-hand quadrant. Draw a long, arcing line counterclockwise, parallel to your first three lines, from the dot in the lower right-hand quadrant all the way around to the bottom of the vertical line. When you have completed this connection, you're done. You've made the outer wall and entrance to your right-handed, classical three-circuit labyrinth.

Use the seed patterns to practice drawing patterns that turn to the right. Since the leftward path is most common, it is helpful to make and trace right-hand labyrinths so that you can use labyrinth drawings to balance yourself like the woman in the story below.

LESSONS OF THE LABYRINTH

A woman I know keeps a labyrinth meditation notebook by her bed. Every night, before going to sleep, she draws left- and right-handed three-circuit labyrinths. She draws them on facing pages of her notebook, then traces the paths with her finger on the finished drawings. She repeats the process in the morning. She switches every day so that each hand walks a different path every day. One day the right hand will walk the right-handed labyrinth and the left hand will walk the left-handed labyrinth. The next day, she will reverse the order, so that the right hand walks the left-handed labyrinth and the left hand walks the right-handed labyrinth. She calls the practice "Morning Pilgrimage" and "Evening Pilgrimage." The practice balances her energies and is important to her sense of well-being.

Walking Two Labyrinths Simultaneously

One evening, some friends and I had an interesting realization. It occurred after we had drawn right- and left-handed labyrinths and tried to walk them simultaneously, one hand per labyrinth. One friend found it to be an almost insurmountable task. She quickly recognized that this exercise was challenging her to center herself—to balance her right and left brain—in a completely different way than walking the full-size labyrinth, since it's impossible to walk two large labyrinths simultaneously. She believes that the degree of difficulty you experience can indicate how far out of balance you may be in certain aspects of your life.

Another friend carries a notebook whenever she travels. In the notebook, she has drawn left- and right-handed labyrinths on facing pages. Like many people, she finds walking the two labyrinths simultaneously to be a dauntingly challenging task. Perhaps because it is so tricky, she finds it to be an especially effective tool. Walking the two labyrinths seems to help her stay balanced, no matter what the situation. Oftentimes, she walks the labyrinths before going into important meetings.

'Til turning, turning, we come round right.
—From the Shaker hymn "Simple Gifts"

Drawing a Left-Handed Seven-Circuit Labyrinth

Once you're comfortable with drawing the basic, classical three-circuit labyrinth, you're ready to move on to drawing a classical seven-circuit labyrinth. You start a seven-circuit labyrinth with the same steps as the three-circuit labyrinth. First draw two lines of each length—one vertical, the other horizontal—that cross each other at their midpoints. Then draw four dots in the upper of the four quadrants, as you did with the three-circuit labyrinth.

Be sure to position the cross in the lower middle of the page—even more than with the three-circuit labyrinth, you're going to need the room. In a seven-circuit labyrinth, you're going to be creating a total of eight concentric walls. As with the three-circuit labyrinth, they grow larger at the top than at the bottom.

The next step in creating a seven-circuit labyrinth is one that is not in the three-circuit labyrinth. Notice, once again, that in drawing the cross you have created four quadrants. Within each quadrant, draw a right-angle "L" just inside the quadrant, with the lines of the L parallel to the vertical and horizontal lines. The lines should be equidistant from the main cross and the dot.

Next, starting from the top of the vertical line of the center cross, draw an arc with your pencil clockwise to the top of the floating angle's vertical line in the upper right-hand quadrant.

Then, pick up your pencil and move it to the upper left-hand quadrant to the top of the vertical line in the floating angle. From the top of the vertical line in the floating angle, draw an arcing line, roughly parallel to the first line, to the dot in the corner of the upper right-hand quadrant. (Hint: In creating a left-handed labyrinth, you always trace your arcing line from the next open dot or line on your left clockwise to the next open dot or line on the right.)

Next, go to the dot in the upper left-hand quadrant. From this dot, draw a long, arcing line, parallel to your first two arcs, to the end of the horizontal line in the right angle in the upper right-hand quadrant.

From the left end or the horizontal in the floating angle in the upper left-hand quadrant, draw a line extending the horizontal out to the left one path width and then continue an arcing line, parallel to your previous arcs, up and to the right end of the horizontal line of the main cross.

Go to the left end of the horizontal line of the main cross, extend it out to the left, and draw a long arcing line, parallel to your previous arcs, to the right end of the horizontal line in the floating angle in the lower right-hand quadrant.

Now, go to the dot in the lower left-hand quadrant. Draw a long, curving line, parallel to your previous arcs, all the way around to the bottom of the vertical line in the floating angle in the lower right quadrant.

Go to the left end of the horizontal line of the floating angle in the lower left-hand quadrant and draw a long, curving line, parallel to the previous arcs, all the way around to the dot in the lower right-hand quadrant.

You're almost done. Only two more lines to go. Go to the dot in the lower left-hand quadrant; draw a long, arcing line, parallel to your previous arcs, all the way around the labyrinth to the bottom of the vertical line of the floating angle in the lower right-hand quadrant. Now all you have left is the outer wall. Go to the bottom of the vertical line in the floating angle in the lower left-hand quadrant, extend it downward one path width, and then draw a long, curving line, parallel to your previous arcs, all the way around and up to the bottom of the vertical line of the central cross. You're done.

You're created a classical seven-circuit labyrinth. Before practicing drawing more of them, you may want to "walk" the path with your finger and savor your accomplishment. Notice that you start by going up into the middle of the labyrinth, then swing to the outside of the labyrinth, before finally circling back to the center. This is the 3-2-1-4-7-6-5-8 pathway (with "8" as the center) that we described on page 106. Trace the turns and counterturns of this pathway, even with a pencil, marker, or finger, and I think you'll feel not only a surge of accomplishment but also a sense of the energy of the labyrinth. From simple, everyday tools—a pencil and paper—you've re-created a thousands-of-years-old meditation tool.

Often when teaching Sunday school classes about labyrinths and after walking one with the kids, I like to teach them how to draw one. They seem to really love it. Some get it right away; most think it's pretty cool to be able to draw a labyrinth, especially after having just completed a walk. I often teach older children how to draw both the left- and right-handed labyrinths. Sometimes I show them how to expand into bigger labyrinths. (Any of the basic seed patterns can be expanded by adding an additional "L" right angle in each quadrant.) If there's a piano nearby, we try to pick out the tune of the labyrinth (another discovery of my friend Sig Lonegren), since walking the paths of the seven-circuit labyrinth in the order 3-2-1-4-7-6-5-8 translates to a perfect piano octave: E-D-C-F-B-A-G-(high) C.

Drawing a Right-Handed Seven-Circuit Labyrinth

Now that you know how to draw a left-handed seven-circuit labyrinth, let's do a right-handed one. The first two steps are the same first two steps of the other labyrinths you have learned by now. First, draw a vertical line and a horizontal line of equal lengths that intersect at their midpoints. Then put dots in the far corners of the four quadrants that are created by the cross. The third step is the same as the third step in the left-handed seven-circuit labyrinth: Within each of the four quadrants, equidistant from the midpoint of the center cross and the dot in the quadrant's corner, draw a floating, 90-degree angle composed of a vertical and horizontal line.

Now continue to connect each of the elements the same way, drawing each of your arcs to the left, counterclockwise, beginning at the top of the cross.

Since drawing counterclockwise can be a challenge, you probably will want to draw several right-handed labyrinths as practice. But be sure and take the time to "walk" the labyrinth. Just as it feels unusual to draw in a counterclockwise direction, it probably will also feel a bit strange to follow the right-handed labyrinth, with its paths going in the opposite direction. As you continue to draw and walk these labyrinths, and use them as part of your spiritual practice, you might have surprising insights as you move in this "counterintuitive" direction. For now, walking the labyrinth's path also should reinforce your sense of accomplishment. In the course of these few pages, you've learned how to create a thing of beauty. Again, congratulations! Use the seed patterns to practice drawing right-handed labyrinths.

Drawing a Classical Five-Circuit Labyrinth

Now that you know the trick to drawing classical three-circuit and seven-circuit labyrinths, how do you think you might draw a classical five-circuit one? You begin with a variation of the classical seed pattern, but there are two options. First, you can draw the seed pattern with the pair of floating angles in the top half, leaving them off in the bottom half. Or, you can leave the angles off in the top half but include them in the bottom half. Experiment with each of these and see which version is most appealing to you. Five-circuit labyrinths are not very common, yet they come in handy when you need to work in a small space and don't have room to make a full-size seven-circuit.

The great Tao flows everywhere, to the left and to the right.
—Tao-Te Ching

Walking the Finger or Drawn Labyrinth

Walking a tabletop or hand-drawn labyrinth is not like the old Yellow Pages ads: You don't just "let your fingers do the walking." You bring your full attention to it, as you do when you walk a full-size labyrinth. Before starting, you may want to compose an intention. If you walk a finger labyrinth before going into a business meeting, you may want to seek guidance on the meeting generally or on a specific issue or dynamic that you anticipate will come up in the meeting. If you walk a finger labyrinth before going to bed, you may want to use it to let go of events of the day—or, alternatively, to focus on something that you want to dream about. Waking up in the morning, you may want to walk your finger labyrinth as an exercise—like meditation, yoga, or saying a prayer—to center yourself and open yourself to what lies before you in the day ahead.

As when you walk a full-size labyrinth, if you are present in the moment, you also will be more conscious of the walk itself. Are you rushing to the center? Is the labyrinth bringing up feelings that you need to be dealing with in your life? What's it like to be on the path, winding back and forth; to be in the center; to be on the path back? How is it similar to and different from walking a full-size labyrinth? You may want to have an affirmation or meditation as you walk the labyrinth. You may find that some mantras work particularly well for armchair labyrinth walking. If you are walking two labyrinths simultaneously, with both hands, you may—like my friends—experience something completely different from what you feel when walking a single labyrinth.

Labyrinths in Living Color

What color is your labyrinth? It's not such a far-fetched question. With color, you can add a new dimension, and perhaps learn something about yourself in the process.

Labyrinths can be painted using any colors you like in any way you wish to use them. Classical seven-circuit labyrinths are frequently rainbow colored as the seven paths correspond so well with the seven colors of the rainbow. If you want to use your labyrinth for problem solving as explained on page 141, you will need to use the colors in order, beginning with red on the outer path and ending with violet on the inner path. You can use either black or white for the center.

There are two ways to paint a labyrinth with the rainbow colors. The most popular is to color the pathways so that you are actually walking on the color or tracing your finger directly on it.

When I designed the classical seven-circuit rainbow labyrinth for the Labyrinth Project of Connecticut, I wasn't happy with the idea of walking directly on the painted canvas. I wasn't sure how the paint would hold up over time and I couldn't decide exactly where one path ended and the next one began. I started playing around with my children's crayons and came up with the idea of coloring the walls instead of the paths. I think the rainbow labyrinth I created is far more elegant and it works just as well. There is no question which color path you are on in my design and the walls all have neat and tidy beginnings and endings where the colors can be mitered together.

Each wall is made up of two lines of different colors. For simplicity we will refer to them as the inside and the outside lines of the walls. The only design choice is whether to make the outside wall a single red line or a double one. We decided to make ours a single line.

In any case, follow this procedure to color your rainbow labyrinth:

LESSONS FROM THE LABYRINTH

Once you know the basics of making a labyrinth, imagination can take over. When Robert Ferré was asked to create a labyrinth in a school gym, his idea at first was to make the labyrinth pattern on the floor using masking tape. However, when he arrived at the school, he saw that the hallways were full of bags of canned goods that had been collected for a food drive. As he made his way to the gym, he asked students to bring along the bags. When they got to the gym, they started creating the labyrinth using cans. By the time they were done, they had created a distinctive labyrinth out of Campbell's soup, Spaghetti-O's, and cans of vegetables and fruits in every color of the rainbow.

Cathie LeVasseur drew mirror images of the seven-circuit labyrinth in chalk on her driveway. After she had finished, she decided to use her child's toy cars to traverse the labyrinth because the driveway was too rough on her finger. "The cars fit perfectly into the width of the path," she said, "and they were the right size for my hand to hold. The funny thing was, my son came out and wanted to use the labyrinth as a race-track for his cars. In fact, we made a bigger one in our backyard just the right size for him to ride his Tonka toy around!"

1. Make your outside wall red.

2. Make the second wall red on the outside and orange on the inside.

3. Make the third wall orange on the outside and yellow on the inside.

4. Make the fourth wall yellow on the outside and green on the inside.

5. Make the fifth wall green on the outside and blue on the inside.

6. Make the sixth wall blue on the outside and purple on the inside.

7. Make the seventh wall purple on the outside and violet on the inside.

8. Make the eighth wall violet on the outside and either black or white on the inside.

(We used black as it is the combination of all colors and because it stands out well against the cream-colored background of the canvas.)

A Connecticut seven-circuit, showing inside and outside colored walls.

HELEN CURRY

You will notice that both sides of the outer path are red. It has become the "red path" because you are walking between two red lines that radiate the color red from both sides. This path has the energy of the color red. And so it is for each of the seven paths and for the center. They now vibrate to the frequency of their own color, just as musical notes each vibrate to a different frequency.

As you walk your colored labyrinth, see if you can feel the difference between the energies of the colors. Notice if you are particularly drawn to one or more of them. Do you feel any sensations in areas of your body as you move from one color to the next? Do you sense that the whole labyrinth has a new kind of energy or pulse as a result of the rainbow colors?

Even the act of coloring your labyrinth can bring up intense feelings. You might feel a physical sensation in different parts of your body while you are drawing. I experienced this firsthand one night as my friends and I drew labyrinths together. We decided to color the drawings. As I began to add colors, I started to feel vibrations. I had a sense of the energy moving up my torso as I went from coloring the outer path of the labyrinth red through coloring each successive path with the colors of the rainbow. When I walked the labyrinth with my finger, I felt a definite tingling in my hands. Like my friends' earlier discoveries drawing counterclockwise and walking two labyrinths simultaneously, it was a revelation. With just paper, pencils, colors, and presence of mind, we had tapped into a fascinating phenomenon.

Chakras and Colors

To many people, the seven paths of the classical seven-circuit labyrinth, in combination with the center, can represent a "map" of the energy centers of our bodies, called chakras. Chakras—the seven energy centers of the human body in yoga philosophy—are thought of as centers of the different vibrations. People call these energies "chi" or "prana," depending on their particular tradition. Many people feel there is a connection between energy centers and various colors of the rainbow. Labyrinth followers have used the rainbow colors on the paths of the labyrinth to conform to the colors of the chakras. Doing so enables you to focus on the body's energy centers as you follow the path of the labyrinth.

The first chakra is the "root" and it is located at the base of the spine. It vibrates to the frequency of the color red. It reflects our physical body and is our connection with three-dimensional reality. It also reflects our "roots" overall, such as our earliest memories and connections.

The second chakra, moving up the spine, is the sacral chakra, which is two inches below the navel. It has the frequency of the color orange. The sacral chakra is associated with the bones in the spine called the sacrum, the place where lower back pain often appears. It's also associated with the spleen, or spleenic center, in the front of the torso. This center holds our emotional, sexual, and creative energies.

The lumbar or solar plexus chakra is the third chakra. It is our power center and is considered to be the place where the ego resides. It is associated with the color yellow and is the seat of our intellect and our mental energies.

The fourth chakra is the heart or dorsal energy center chakra, which is supposed to be the perfectly balanced chakra. It's the center chakra: There are three chakras above it and three chakras below it. The heart chakra is the place for the beginnings of spiritual paths, including compassion for one's self, others, the planet, and all living creatures. Its color is green.

The throat or cervical chakra is the next, or fifth, chakra. This chakra maintains the energies for further spiritual development, particularly those associated with communicating. Its color is blue. It is said that problems in this area, such as sore throats, are the result of our not speaking our truth.

The third-eye chakra comes next. It is the sixth chakra, and is located on the forehead above and between our eyes. The third-eye chakra is the center of Christ-consciousness. It's the place where energy connections and communications with higher consciousness transpire. This chakra is associated with the color indigo or purple and is the place of our intuition.

The seventh and final chakra is the crown chakra. It's also called the wisdom chakra. It's located at the top of the head, and is associated with the Divine or the "All That Is." It is associated with the color violet or magenta.

There are many resources on chakra energies and their related colors, both in bookstores and on the World Wide Web.

Creating Three-Dimensional Labyrinths

Can you think of any flat surfaces—traditional or not—that you would like to infuse with the power of the sacred symbol of the labyrinth? You can put labyrinths on literally anything. You can print labyrinths on T-shirts. You can paint them onto canvases, walls, or tiles. You can lay labyrinths on the earth or carve them out of sand at the beach.

Once you have started drawing labyrinths, you may find that sometimes you would like to close your eyes as you trace it. Normally, closing your eyes won't work: You can't do it on a full-size labyrinth since, unless you were clairvoyant, you'd run into people. And drawn labyrinths don't have the texture to allow you to finger-walk them with your eyes closed. However, a finger-labyrinth board, like the ones I described earlier in this chapter, would certainly meet the need. It's not hard to make your own three-dimensional or raised-surface labyrinth. Building your own lets your customize the labyrinth—and it's fun!

Do you want to be able to carry the labyrinth around with you? If so, be sure to pick a material that is light enough for you to carry comfortably. If it doesn't need to be portable, is there a special place that you want to put your labyrinth? Do you want your labyrinth to be, or be part of, an altar? As you select your materials, remember that you can add to the sense that you are creating a sacred space by blessing the materials you are using. (For more on blessings, see page 154.)

As with walking a labyrinth, it's important to be mindful when you create a labyrinth. Without mindful intention, the power of the labyrinth—like the power of all spiritual practices—can dissipate.

You need to find a flat surface for your labyrinth. Perhaps you have a piece of plywood or a tray that you can use. Maybe a space in your home—a shelf, countertop, or dresser top—would make a good sacred spot for your labyrinth. Potters or people with access to slabs of clay may want to work in that material, using a clay tablet and indenting pathways or building clay walls on the surface. After you have your material, work on it so it will be smooth to the touch. For example, if you're working with wood, you may want to sand it and finish it to eliminate splinters.

Once your materials are ready, draw your seed pattern onto your base. Before drawing, think about what kind of labyrinth you want: a three-circuit, seven-circuit, or other pattern. Do you want it to be left-handed or right-handed, or will you do both? You may want to draw several kinds of labyrinths on paper and trace them with your finger to see which pattern you are most drawn to. Think, also, about how large you want your labyrinth to be. Do you want it to cover as much of the base as possible? Or do you want to leave a border around the labyrinth? Also think of the material you will be working with. You need to allow for wider walls if you are using shells, for example, than you would if you were using a line of glue.

There are so many materials you can use to build your raised-edge labyrinth. Small stones make a historically appropriate material for your labyrinth walls.

With a strong adhesive (you may want to try several kinds of glue on test boards before going to the real thing), you can glue the stones along the walls of the labyrinth. Shells, crystals, seeds, pine cones, and other objects from nature are also nice materials for this purpose. Alternatively, you may want to make the labyrinth truly yours by using special things that you have collected over the years—buttons, for instance.

You may want to build your labyrinth out of papier-mâché, which is easy to paint. There are also new kinds of modeling materials in art supply and craft stores, such as gauze-infused plasterlike materials, that are great for labyrinth building. These materials, which are often used in making masks are easy to use and harden quickly. Bear in mind, though, that you'll probably need to build a structure underneath the modeling material so that it will keep its shape.

On the other hand, you can create an easy—and colorful—labyrinth by tracing the outline of the labyrinth with a thick stream of glue and dropping materials like sand (colored, store-bought, or collected at the beach) into the glue. The hardened glue and sand combination is just textured enough so you can easily follow the path of the labyrinth. Of course, you don't have to use sand. You can use glitter, yarn, velvet cord—whatever speaks to you.

I've heard of people making labyrinths out of all kinds of things. See what you have around: Play-Doh from when the kids were little? Twine? Modeling clay? Even if you don't have an artistic bent, you've probably made "snakes" with clay. It's one of those instinctive reactions when you have a piece of clay in your hands: You roll it out until it has a ropelike shape. These snakes and ropes can—in the hands of the labyrinth walker—be the beginnings of the walls for your labyrinth.

As you make your labyrinth come to life, think about the process. Are you learning anything about yourself? Try walking your three-dimensional labyrinth.

Walk it with your eyes closed. Does it change the quality or nature of the experience for you? If so, what's different? After you've walked the labyrinth a couple of times, do you begin to anticipate its twists and turns? Is the labyrinth pattern starting to be imprinted in your memory?

Children with finger labyrinths.

JOEL BERRY

CHAPTER 9

The Healing Labyrinth

Everything revolves. Revolution is the basic movement of all life.
—Neale Donald Walsch
Conversations with God

It should be no surprise that, as their popularity grows, more people are using labyrinths to address specific health problems. There are few treatments that work on all levels—body, mind, emotions, spirit—like the labyrinth does. I have met people who walk the labyrinth for a specific medical reason, from preparation for surgery to recovery to treatment of chronic illness. Many formulate a specific intention related to their problem before starting their walk, asking for guidance on how to be strong, put their anxieties aside, and have a successful procedure. Many try to find an appropriate affirmation, mantra, or phrase to repeat during the walk. One woman, who had done a labyrinth walk in preparation for surgery, wrote to me after her operation: "It was an exquisite walk, and I felt very centered and very calm even though I was to have surgery the following week," she wrote. The feelings of being centered and "turned in on myself," she said, "stayed with me through the week, up to and including the operation."

She believes the labyrinth walk helped speed her recovery. After the surgery, she reported, she felt "incredible strength." She found another unexpected benefit as well: "Although I'd had painkillers during the procedure, I discovered I did not need any more during the recovery process."

Not everyone has such unqualified success. But most report feeling calmer and more centered going into or recovering from surgery because they have walked a labyrinth. And some in the medical professions have found that the labyrinth can produce other breakthroughs. One friend who has been using finger labyrinths with children persuaded a pediatrician to place a labyrinth board in the waiting room. The children thought it was another toy, but the labyrinth began making a difference. One parent called me to say that his son normally gets "utterly terrified" at the prospect of going to the doctor. When they got to the doctor's office they found the finger labyrinth, and, together, began tracing its path, the boy sitting on his father's lap. "He got totally distracted from his fear and absorbed in the textures and paths," his father said. The anxiety stayed at bay when they went into the doctor's office.

Labyrinth Society member Victoria Stone built the labyrinth at San Francisco's California Pacific Medical Center, one of the first hospital labyrinths in the country. She reports that a number of people at the medical center walk the labyrinth to support their healing process. Some walk it before radiation or chemotherapy to ground themselves and focus their energy for healing. The chaplains have a prayer walk every Friday afternoon as a ritual to support the health and healing of all the patients, families, and staff at the medical center.

One afternoon, a family member of a patient (someone that one of the chaplains had been counseling earlier in the day) noticed the chaplains' labyrinth prayer walk through the waiting room windows (the labyrinth is located outside the hospital entrance adjacent to the waiting area). She saw this vision as a positive sign and decided to join in the walk. Earlier in the day this women had been quite distraught about her daughter's condition. After the labyrinth walk she told the chaplain counseling her that, in watching the chaplains walking the labyrinth, she experienced a sense that all would be well. It was uplifting to her just seeing this ritual, and the walk provided her with a feeling of peace and freedom from all her worries. She said she felt much more hope about the outcome of her daughter's illness. Her chaplain said that the labyrinth walk had done more for this woman than anything else that had been done for her that day.

Labyrinths and Therapy

People are using labyrinths in therapeutic settings all over the world. Some of our most enthusiastic advocates are the Russian psychotherapists, family counselors, and art therapists who attend the annual Conference on Creativity, the Arts, and Spirituality in the Healing Professions sponsored by the Harmony Institute in St. Petersburg, Russia, each summer. Elaine Foster and I introduced the labyrinth for the first time in Russia at that conference in 1995, and we have had a member of the Labyrinth Society bring a labyrinth every summer since. Now at least one family counselor in Russia uses the labyrinth every day in her work with troubled children.

A regular attendee at my public walks once expressed gratitude for the walks, which he said had become a lifeline to him as he began a twelve-step recovery program. He explained, "I was introduced to the labyrinth walks at the same time that I made a commitment to get clean. In those early days, I was in the first stage of recovery, where you go to 90 meetings in 90 days. It is one of the first and most significant time frames in recovery. The labyrinth walks that you sponsored seemed to be once every 90 days or so. They became a lifeline for me, and a chance to mark these 90-day cycles."

Just as the goal for those in recovery is taking it one day at a time, the labyrinth makes such a commitment concrete by helping them one step at a time.

One of our board members has her son "walk" a finger labyrinth with both his hands to increase his concentration before starting his homework, and a local Montessori school has put a seven-circuit labyrinth on their front lawn so that the students can walk it whenever they like.

Neal Harris's Intuipath finger labyrinth is designed for the therapist and patient to walk simultaneously at the outset of or during their session. Neal, a licensed clinical counselor and fellow member of the Labyrinth Society, says the Intuipath is based on the premise that quieting the mind and slowing down the body through relaxation enhances the interpersonal and intrapersonal communications that are the basis of therapy. The idea is that, as client and therapist walk the labyrinth, they become more comfortable and more intuitively "linked in" to each other.

Animals and the Labyrinth

Labyrinths seem to be equally therapeutic for animals. I read an article by Jean Lutz in her no-longer-published newsletter *The Labyrinth Letter* about a group in New Mexico that is using the labyrinth to promote healing, training, and communication with animals through the use of a technique called the Tellington Touch. "Practitioners have been using the meander path, or

LESSONS FROM THE LABYRINTH

In a relaxation class Neal Harris was teaching on how to use a finger labyrinth, one middle-aged woman reported that she had been told that morning that she was being let go from a job that she had held for almost 25 years. She stated how angry and frustrated this made her feel, and, as a result, her plan was to walk out of the class a few minutes after it started. She was so upset that she couldn't sit still, but as she began running her finger through the design, a tiny edge of her anger seemed to leave her, so she continued to trace the design with her finger. As she came close to the center of the design, she heard this voice inside her that said, "Now you will have the time that you need in order to take your grandchild to the pool this summer." She said that at that moment, in the blink of an eye, all of her anger left her. She revealed that this was an answer to an issue that she had been praying about for months: "How can I spend more time with my grandchild and not miss his formative years because of my heavy work schedule." With the layoff, now she could! What a powerful and elegant tool for personal peace and transformation.

labyrinth, as they refer to it, in their revolutionary work with animals of all kinds," Lutz writes. There is a photograph of a German shepherd with hip dysplasia and a tendency to pull on the leash "who learns to stay with the leader and to focus" by using the labyrinth. The article goes on to describe the extraordinary work they are doing with horses and says, "Horses have been observed walking a labyrinth on their own when one is left in the field." I, for one, can believe it.

Once I got a call during the afternoon before a public walk from a woman who said that she wanted to walk the labyrinth, but she was housesitting for a dog and she didn't want to leave the dog at home. Nor did she feel she could leave the dog out in the car.

Well, if our rules include people taking their shoes off to walk the labyrinth, you can imagine my reaction to the thought of a dog on the labyrinth. Don't misunderstand. I own two beloved dogs, but I wouldn't dream of risking what they might do to my beloved labyrinth! I offered her the option of parking right in front at the door of the church in the handicapped parking area. I promised to have the volunteers check on the dog while she was walking. Although she said she might consider that option, she still wanted to bring the dog with her on her labyrinth walk.

I said, with ill-disguised panic, "Are you going to walk with the dog on a leash?"

She said, "No, I am going to carry the dog. It's a small dog."

In the end, I acquiesced. "But if it yaps, you are out of there," I said. She did indeed show up with a small, white, fluffy, very well behaved dog. It sat quietly in her arms the whole time she was walking, looking sweet and peeking around. Everybody in the church noticed, and some walkers assumed the dog was ill and needed the healing power of the labyrinth. I think most appreciated the dog's loving energy.

Labyrinths for Caregivers

Labyrinth walking can be beneficial for caregivers as well as patients. I once conducted a workshop for the staff and administration of a hospice. There is a tremendous amount of burnout in people who work in these facilities, where patients are close to the end of their lives. Anything that alleviates stress is truly valuable. Both staff and administrators participated in the walk, and they loved it. As they walked the labyrinth and then shared their stories, a number of the walkers were really moved. There was a palpable change in the room. Many participants expressed interest in having a permanent labyrinth at the facility. One woman felt the labyrinth was a perfect metaphor for hospice work, as the path can stand for the walk through life and toward death.

I conducted a similar workshop at a nursing home in New Jersey. The workshop was open to spiritual counselors and pastors of nursing homes throughout the county. The day was designed to be a nurturing experience for the 50 or so clergy and pastoral volunteers who attended. Oftentimes groups like this end up giving so much to the people they serve that they don't take time to nurture themselves. Walking our big Chartres-style labyrinth, talking about the great pilgrimage cathedrals of Europe, was restorative. For once, they didn't have to give. Instead, they could receive.

Labyrinth Work in Prisons

In the winter of 1995, the Dominican Sisters in Sparkill, New York, wrote in their newsletter, *Weavings*, about a labyrinth I had built for their retreat center. In the corner of the first page of the newsletter, they reproduced a tiny, 1¼-inch image of the Chartres labyrinth.

The image caught the attention of a prison inmate who found a copy of the newsletter. He tried to imagine what it would be like to walk the labyrinth. As he described it in a letter to Sister Adele of the Dominican Sisters, he said he was not sure what he would think about if he were walking the labyrinth. "Perhaps I would concentrate on just getting to the center," he said. He thought he probably would watch the changing perspective of the scenery, and only watch the brick path peripherally, as that was his practice in his walks

The spirit always finds a pathway. . . . If you find a deer trail and follow that trail, it's going to lead you to medicines and waterholes and a shelter.
—WALLACE BLACK ELK
THE SACRED WAYS OF A LAKOTA

LESSONS FROM THE LABYRINTH

Victoria Stone, who built the first hospital labyrinth, told a beautiful story of how it had become an important resource for a paramedic in the San Francisco Fire Department as well as for her colleagues. The paramedic told her there are days when she sees more death and destruction in a twelve-hour period than most people will see in their lifetimes and it affects her deeply. She said that while her professionalism never slips during her shift, she has spent her share of time crying in bathrooms after delivering people to the hospital emergency room hanging on to life by a thread.

For nine years she has been trying to find an easy way to deal with her work-related grief. She was delighted when a labyrinth was placed at California Pacific Medical Center. She said it is hard to describe the peace it brings to her and how it helps get her thoughts in perspective while walking it alone at night after her graveyard shift; she finds a renewal of energy and a release of anxiety that doesn't occur with simple walking. She has, with some effort, gotten some of her more macho coworkers to use the labyrinth and felt she had made tremendous headway when she found one of them using it voluntarily after a particularly bad call. She just fell in behind him on the path. He waited in the middle and they talked about the call. Then she walked back out, leaving him alone at the center with his thoughts.

around the prison yard. "I don't deny the existence of a wall or fence," he says. "But it does not block my view of the river." He'd probably walk the path several times "for the challenge of doing it as physical exercise," he felt. But gradually, he thought, the walk would shift to "a more pure spirituality."

Inspired by thinking about what the walk would be like, he took out a sewing needle and tried to trace the path on the tiny image. Twice, he said, his "bifocal-dependent eyes" led him partway to the center only to wind up back at the beginning. Refusing to give up, he took a pencil and marked his progress. On the third try, he reached the center. He learned a secret along the way, he added: "One comes close to the petals of the center quickly, but then moves farther away until the way returns to the petals and enters them."

After reading this letter, we decided that the Labyrinth Project of Connecticut should start a labyrinth prison ministry. It took several years to arrange, but we now bring a labyrinth two Wednesdays a month to the Federal Correctional Institution at Danbury, Connecticut, for the inmates to walk.

The prison workshops are sponsored by the chaplain's office and usually involve 30 to 40 women inmates. Going to the prison is extraordinary. Each member of the Labyrinth Project of Connecticut who volunteers to go—usually three or four of us—leaves feeling she received more than she had given.

The prison ministry is different from a regular workshop. Generally, in group settings, the goal is to introduce the labyrinth, give the history and background, and provide an opportunity to walk it. Since 70 to 80 percent of the prison walkers come every month, we don't need to introduce them to the experience. Instead, we try to create opportunities for the women to be heard—and to experience silence. They are encouraged to honor their own religious and spiritual traditions.

At the session, everyone sits in chairs in a circle with the labyrinth folded up. After introductions—hugs, pats on the shoulder, and greeting people by name—we go around the circle, asking the participants to tell us their names and anything they would like us to know. Everyone gets an opportunity to share. Sometimes there's a new grandchild. Sometimes there is news that someone will soon be released. One woman reported she was being released and was returning to her family in Europe. She said the second Wednesday labyrinth program had been so important to her that she would mark her calendar and her clock to be with us in spirit every month after she was released.

Each month we offer a program that we think might be enriching. We generally do something relating to the season or holidays in that month, often something very simple. In the fall, we passed around a couple of leaves beginning to turn colors. We wanted to suggest the image of transition within the leaf, and to use the idea of transition to get them to start to talk. Sometimes we share poetry. Occasionally, we have read some scripture. Around Mother's Day, we might ask them to remember something about their mothers to share with us. We have also offered information about chakras, ideas about energy, and suggestions for various meditations.

Next, we stack up the chairs and unfold the labyrinth. We stand in a circle, hold hands, and bless the labyrinth. That blessing ceremony has always included the powers of the four directions, with four directional candles, each lit by one of the inmates. We ask that divine light and love be present in the space and on the pathways and in the center of the labyrinth. We ask also that each of us be blessed in our journeys. We then walk the labyrinth, turning down the lights as much as we can and playing quiet music. It is a precious time. They walk. They sit. They try not to talk. They meditate. They pray—they even sleep.

We also offer feather blessings (see page 154), or chakra cleansing, or hands-on healing. Every now and then, I will hand the feather to one of the inmates and ask her to bless me. After all, I don't have any special powers that they don't have, and I want to empower them. In many ways, the workshop has become much more of an exchange over the years. Now we sometimes invite the inmates to design the programs for us.

After the hour for the actual labyrinth walk is up, we form a circle to offer everyone an opportunity to share her experiences, and talk some more. Sometimes someone will share something quite profound. It might be as simple as "I felt the presence" to "I understand why my life took the direction that it did." We then go into a closing ceremony in which everybody offers one word. In the beginning, I expected to hear the word "freedom" a lot in this ceremony. But it is rarely used. Instead, we hear words like *joy, peace, love, friendship, gratitude, happiness*—words that you might be surprised to hear from incarcerated women.

Using the Labyrinth in Problem Solving

As I've said before, labyrinth walking is an exceptionally good way to achieve clarity. Using phrases like "I am a Pilgrim seeking . . ." can help you take large steps toward defining what you want. If you can't finish the phrase because you're not sure what you want, you can take the idea of the phrase with you as you go. As you proceed, you may find the clarity that has eluded you.

In this problem-solving model, it does not matter what labyrinth you walk. The solution to the problem lies in restating the question or restating the issue in such a way that you get clarity about what you want.

Here are some questions to ask yourself as you begin to have a clearer sense of your intention:

Now that I know what I want, how can I get from here to there?
What are my next steps?
What are the obstacles?
What did I need to do?
What am I trying to create here?

As you continue the walk, think of your steps on the labyrinth as the steps you must take. You might look at the turns of the labyrinth as metaphors for the roadblocks you have in your life. Think about how you can expand the

A very important image in a difficult relationship came to consciousness, and I am grateful.
—Book of Reflections

possibilities when you look at the blocks as simply turns in the path. They may be 180-degree turns, but they can't *stop* you. They don't stand in the way of your forward movement; they simply send you off in a new direction.

The Labyrinth and Dreams

Using the labyrinth in combination with your dreams gives you even more opportunity to connect with your own inner knowledge—what you don't even know that you know. The labyrinth will help you access those buried insights and give you guidance on solving your problem.

As you get ready to go to sleep, identify an issue that you want to clarify. State specifically what the issue is. If you keep a labyrinth journal, write down your intention and problem. Then, walk a finger labyrinth or hand-drawn labyrinth at bedtime, before going to sleep. You might walk both left- and right-handed labyrinths simultaneously, in order to come up with a solution that reflects a positive balance between the rational and the intuitive sides of the brain.

If a specific thought occurs to you as you do the finger-walk, make a note to yourself but keep an open mind for any additional insights that may come up while you sleep. In the morning, write down everything you can recall—dreams, fragments, images, thoughts, impressions, inspirations. Leave these notes to look at later.

Reflect on what came up at the bedtime finger-walk the night before. Is there anything in your dreams that helps you clarify the problem? If you don't feel that you got the guidance you were looking for, try the process for three nights in a row. Ask for insights to take you deeper into the problem. As you go along, review your notes. You probably will see a progression of insight and themes that recur in your dreams. Within this, you may find an answer emerging.

Advanced Problem Solving

When the Labyrinth Project of Connecticut invited Sig Lonegren to give a workshop presenting his problem-solving method, our first order of business was to create a seven-circuit labyrinth on canvas and paint it the colors of the rainbow, as described on page 120. Having the smaller labyrinth opened up opportunities for us to give walks and workshops in spaces that weren't large enough for our Chartres-style labyrinth, thus solving a problem for the Labyrinth Project of Connecticut!

In his workshop, and in his writings, Sig outlines what I think is a brilliant but somewhat more complex strategy for problem solving than the ones I've described. Sig's problem-solving method involves walking the path of the seven-circuit labyrinth and consciously examining the problem from different perspectives while simultaneously feeling the body's response at each of the body's seven energy centers or chakras.

Since each of the energy centers ties to both a path on the labyrinth as well as a modality of experience in the world, the problem is considered in light of each modality as one walks on that part of the path.

Sig suggests you recognize that you traverse the paths of the seven-circuit labyrinth in a specific order: 3-2-1-4-7-6-5- and 8 (or center), and then back out from 8: 5-6-7-4-1-2-3. Using Sig's model, the third path considers the problem from the power center or solar plexus. This is the rational-thinking modality. So, as you enter the labyrinth on the third path, which is the first path of the labyrinth walk, with the energy of yellow, consider: What do I think about the problem?

My inner child danced your rainbow, the little labyrinth. We tasted each color along the way. Blessings and thanks!

—BOOK OF
REFLECTIONS

As you turn to enter the second path, you enter the realm of feeling and emotion, associated with your sacral center, and with the color orange. Ask: How do I feel about the problem?

As you round the turn to the first or outermost path, you enter the realm of the root or base energy center aligned with the physical realm and the color red. Ask yourself: What are the physical repercussions of this problem? What practical issues such as money are related to the problem?

From the outermost path, you move to the fourth path, connected with the heart center. This reflects the energy of your personal spirituality and of the color green. Ask yourself: How will this problem affect my spiritual life?

From the fourth path, you walk even closer to the center, to path seven. This path connects with your highest energy center, the crown. It reflects the energy of violet. This path relates to union with the Divine. It is along this path that you can open yourself to divine guidance from your highest self, or, in specific terms, ask for God's help if you are comfortable doing that.

Moving from the lofty seventh path, you spiral outward to path six, connected with the third eye's energy center and the color purple or indigo. This path connects you with your vision of the truth as it is related to your problem. It is on this path that the message will come to you or that you will see the truth and will know what the answer to the problem might be for you. You receive the guidance of your intuition.

As you round the turn to path five, you will connect with the energy center of the throat and the color blue. It is the realm of communication with and manifestation from higher spiritual energies. On this path you ask yourself what is your first step now that you have your answer.

From path five, you will move into the center. Be still and clear your mind of all thought. Stay for the space of one breath or just until the next thought comes in and then turn and begin the journey back out, reversing the process. Review each aspect of the problem.

On the fifth path review what your first step will be now that you have the answer. On the sixth path review the answer, message, or vision. On the seventh path thank your deity of choice. On the fourth path review how the answer will affect your spiritual life. On the first path review the practical aspects of the answer. On the second path ask yourself how you feel about the answer. Finally, on the third path ask yourself what you think.

This method isn't easy to remember in the beginning, but after a while you will find that it becomes second nature. As I have Sig's permission to teach this problem-solving model, I usually list these instructions on a large poster that can be easily seen, or I invite the workshop participants to make reminder notes on a small piece of paper to carry with them as they walk.

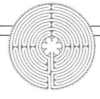

CHAPTER 10

The Ceremonial Labyrinth

It is a walk of love.

—*WALKING IN SACRED CIRCLES*
Labyrinth Project of Connecticut video

A walk of love. The description came from the father of the groom in the first wedding I held on a labyrinth. I think the words describe the possibilities that labyrinths can bring to all sorts of ceremonies. The duality of the labyrinth—connecting the physical act of walking with the inner act of meditation, and the outward journey of our lives with our inner, spiritual passages—resonates with the duality of public ceremonies. A wedding is often called a "public affirmation of a private commitment." Walking the labyrinth in a ceremony can connect you both to the community of friends—

who can witness and acknowledge the event from the perimeter of the circle—and to the larger community of humankind across cultures and generations. For thousands of years, labyrinths have been interwoven into rituals in cultures from Europe to Asia to South and North America.

The idea of using labyrinths in weddings arose soon after I started my labyrinth work. After the second public walk I facilitated, a young man who happened to be the son of a dear friend spoke to me about his girlfriend walking the labyrinth on New Year's Eve 1993. "I realized in that moment, when I saw her at the center, that this was the woman I wanted to marry, and that I wanted to marry her on the labyrinth," he said. At the time, he confided to me, he had not yet asked her to marry him.

Eventually he asked her and she accepted. I worked with the couple for a year and a half; together we created their personal ceremony on the labyrinth. The preparations included painting a special ceremonial three-circuit labyrinth wide enough for them to walk together. At the same time, I was called to be ordained into the interfaith ministry of the Universal Brotherhood Movement, so that I could perform the wedding.

I have gone on to officiate several other weddings on the labyrinth. The couples all have their unique stories. One couple who chose a labyrinth wedding, for example, had had a relationship more than twenty years before. Each had gone on to marry someone else. Through a set of odds-defying circumstances, they met up again and realized they were right for each other. The labyrinth walk that was part of their ceremony seemed to be a metaphor for the twists of fate that brought them together, sent them apart, then brought them together again to marry. As they separately walked the path in, they came close and then walked next to each other. Then their paths would diverge, just as it had happened in their lives.

Wedding labyrinth.

HELEN CURRY

Weddings

Weddings on the labyrinth are wonderful and have a completely different feel than traditional weddings. Rather than the traditional walk down the "straight and narrow" of the church aisle, the couple walk around the paths and turns of the labyrinth—a much more accurate metaphor for the journey they are embarking upon. Where many modern weddings seem to be rushed, the labyrinth wedding slows down time. It also seems to connect the participants and observers to the sacred in a way that many modern weddings don't. It's hard for the bride and groom not to connect to their inner journey as they walk the labyrinth—and it's hard for the observers not to be drawn to the center with them. Traditional weddings are familiar and predictable. Labyrinth weddings are anything but.

My labyrinth wedding ceremony usually starts with the guests seated in chairs forming concentric circles around the labyrinth. Once everyone is seated, I walk into the center to create sacred space. Even if the wedding is in a church, I still feel the need to set sacred space and so I have a reading that I have developed over the years that works very nicely to explain the labyrinth and relate it to the marriage ceremony. It also leads into the image of the circle as it relates to marriage and the rings. The blessing and the labyrinth together emblemize these connections beautifully.

After I have come back out to the entrance again, the groom comes to the entrance of the labyrinth and is blessed by his family as he begins his journey. The blessing can be as simple or as elaborate as they choose to make it. The groom then begins his walk, sometimes in silence, sometimes with music, and sometimes with readings by friends or family members.

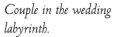

Couple in the wedding labyrinth.

Helen officiating at a labyrinth wedding.

NORTON BERKOWITZ

Sometimes we orchestrate it so that the groom gets to the center before the bride arrives. Sometimes we arrange the groom's walk so that he does not get all the way to the center before the bride arrives. He will have only begun his journey and stopped part way around as she comes to the entrance. He will often just stand still while she is blessed by her family and friends, again as simply or as elaborately as they choose. Now both the bride and groom are walking the labyrinth.

As in life, the two of them have begun their journeys separately; the labyrinth allows this reality to be reflected. At this time they are both moving around in circles, both on the same path, heading to the same place, yet not walking together. They pass each other, which is really powerful because you know they are eventually going to meet. The groom gets to the center. He waits for her. The bride arrives and they come together at the center. Often at this point, there are selected readings by friends or family members. If it's a second marriage for either one of them, and there are children, the children come in. The couple then exchanges their vows.

So far, all the couples have chosen to be in the center by themselves, although there is no particular rule about that, and I could certainly be there with them if they wished. Still, I like the image of them standing alone in the center: They marry each other, I don't marry them.

When the couple walks out together after exchanging vows and rings, it's a lovely image. There is generally music. Some people choose to have additional readings. I meet them at the entrance again for the final blessing.

I love to use the Apache Wedding Blessing (see page 150) because it is gorgeous, resonating with meaning and poetry in a very tender and appropriate way.

There are many variations on this basic outline. At a wedding I officiated in Virginia, the couple wanted the centerpiece of their ceremony to be straight out of the Book of Common Prayer. They created a wonderful opening and closing to make it more personal. Other times, the couples have written the whole ceremony. I think that's appropriate because it's their day. I ask them to reflect on this question: What do you want to say to each other? I have also co-facilitated a wedding with an Episcopal priest. I went in initially, set the sacred space, and stood next to him while he did the traditional Episcopal service. Then I read the Apache Wedding Blessing as the closing prayer.

Now you will feel no rain, for each of you will be shelter to the other. Now you will feel no cold, for each of you will be warmth to the other. Now there is no more loneliness for you, for each of you will be comfort to the other. Though you are two bodies, there is but one life before you. Go now to your dwelling place to enter into the days of your togetherness and may the days of your life be good and long upon the earth. Amen.

—THE APACHE WEDDING BLESSING

Rites of Passage Ceremony

As a society, we are woefully inadequate in creating rituals to symbolize the movement from child to adulthood. There are few opportunities to mark such turnings. Many people are starting to see the need for such traditions, and I contend that the labyrinth is the ideal means to celebrate such occasions. To mark a young girl's thirteenth or sixteenth birthday, or perhaps the onset of her menses, a labyrinth ceremony could involve her mother and any older sisters, any aunts, grandmothers, maybe teachers or older women in the community whom she might look up to. This would be a lovely walk to do with older classmates seated around the circle, and only women in the audience. For a boy's rite of passage, older men, fathers, boys, uncles, and grandfathers could be invited as his council of elders.

Other appropriate occasions to create a labyrinth ceremony include divorce and funerals or memorial services. In the case of a divorce, acknowledging the good while reversing the steps I've outlined for the wedding ceremony, could promote a real mending of wounds. For a memorial labyrinth walk, a symbol of the person you are honoring would be in the center. Family and friends could walk in along the paths and leave a token or a memento at the center. Perhaps they would choose to say something and then walk out. There might be readings, poetry, songs, or stories from the center.

Creating Sacred Space

Creating a sense of the sacred around a labyrinth can make the walk more spiritually meaningful. You might choose to create sacred space around your personal finger-walking experience. Perhaps you have discovered a labyrinth open to the public. How do you make that space sacred for you own walk? Before I begin a labyrinth walk, or even before cleansing the space for the labyrinth prior to blessing it, I like to mentally surround myself in pure white light, which is impervious to all but unconditional love. I ask that everything that follows be only for the highest good.

Some people believe they create a sacred space by clearing energies in a space. There are both inward and outward clearings. First, and most simply, cleansing negative or inharmonious energies in a space can be done by prayer, by creating the intention of clearing.

Combining the inner intention of cleansing with outer signs can be especially effective. There are numerous methods for clearing. Lighting a candle or burning incense or sage, like the Native American smudge stick, can bring cleansing energies. Sometimes people prefer not to burn sage or incense in a group in respect to those with allergies or those who are sensitive to smoke. I often clear a space in the Native American tradition with a feather blessing (see page 154).

Reiki practitioners can bring Reiki energy into the space. A water blessing is lovely, and it connects us with the ancient tradition of using water as a cleansing element. The Catholic Church uses holy water, the small bowl of water can be blessed and sprinkled all around. Using any of the outward signs, space can be cleansed of any negative energy so that divine light and love can be brought in. After clearing and cleansing the space, I then introduce the positive—creating sacred space and inviting in the Divine.

We are born into the world of nature; our second birth is into the world of spirit.
—THE LORD KRISHNA, FROM THE BHAGAVAD GITA

To set the labyrinth itself in a sacred environment, any number of different images can be used. These blessings, rituals, and ceremonies come from a rich and wide variety of traditions, as you will see below. Before a public walks, I always begin with a simple blessing ceremony to create a sacred space, to bless all those who will participate, and to honor walking meditation as a spiritual experience.

I ask for the awareness of the presence of the Divine on the labyrinth. I then ask that the divine light and love be present on the pathways and in the center for all who are gathered and for any people who are yet to come. This is the basis for any creation of sacred space. It's something that can be offered by people either silently to themselves or as part of a blessing ceremony.

No matter where you are putting the labyrinth, even if it is a finger labyrinth just sitting on your knee, if a sacred environment is important to you, then consciously ask that the Divine be present. Alternately, you can ask to be aware of the divine presence on the labyrinth.

If there was ever a space that wasn't sacred to start out with, it was the Norwalk National Guard Armory, where we were painting our first labyrinth on canvas. We had a ten-day span in mid-October 1993, from 7 A.M. to 4 P.M., to work. The floor was horrendously dirty. The sergeant in charge had told me it would be clean, but it wasn't what you or I would think of as clean. Then there was the image of men in jungle fatigues and tanks in the middle of Norwalk, Connecticut, juxtaposed with the Labyrinth Project of Connecticut volunteers, with our new age music and our feather blessings and candles, the floor covered with our canvas and purple paint as we recreated the pattern of the Chartres labyrinth. What a contrast!

We began by blessing the tanks and the dirty floor along with all the labyrinth creators, our materials, the canvas. (I've included that first blessing prayer in the selection of blessings on page 154.) Meanwhile, the sergeant in charge, bless his heart, never smiled. He was the most serious character you have ever seen, straight out of central casting. At one point halfway through the week, we started to challenge ourselves to see who could make him smile. His office was upstairs, and every now and then he would poke his very serious face around the corner. He wasn't distressed by us, he just never smiled. The last day I went in and said good-by to him. He got up, came around the front of his desk, and gave me the biggest hug. I got a sense that much more was going on than just the two of us hugging—two worlds had come together, two whole universes had somehow connected. It just goes to show you, you never know what the labyrinth may bring together.

Our understanding of the sacred leads us back within ourselves. Many people have walked into a space and immediately understood it was sacred. My own feeling is that what you are witnessing is your own inner shift. When you walk into Chartres or Notre Dame or St. John the Divine in New York City, it's instantly a different space than out on the street. But I think the same thing can happen at the ocean or on top of a hill or in the woods or in a special place created in the home.

Closing Sacred Space

I try to keep the closing ceremony very simple. One of my favorites is having everybody stand in a circle and hold hands. Everyone is invited to speak one word. If they choose not to, it's not a problem. They can pass or say it quietly. It's very interesting to hear what people choose when they can only say one word: *thanks, blessings, joy, peace, love, connection, hope, grace.*

Blessing Ceremonies

Ever since the very beginning of my work with labyrinths I have felt that they needed to be blessed before they were walked. The Labyrinth Project of Connecticut, Inc., has held a blessing ceremony before every public walk, and I offer at least a simple blessing at every workshop.

This tradition began for us at the Norwalk Armory. When we gathered there that early October morning in 1993 for the blessing ceremony before beginning our work, I delivered the following prayer:

> *We ask the God of the Universe which knows all, is in all, and is all powerful, to bless this canvas, this beautiful piece of natural cloth soon to be transformed into a sacred object. We ask blessings on the tools and on the paint and on all of the other materials we will use in this project, that they may be put to their highest and best use through the work of our hands. We acknowledge the power of the labyrinth as it was used by the ancient Christians as the completion of their pilgrimages to the great cathedrals of Europe—and, long before that, before recorded history, as it was used in the rites that honored the Goddess. We ask that the presence of all of the spirits back through the ages and forward until the end of time be with us as we now recreate this sacred symbol. Amen.*

In addition to blessing the canvas and the tools, we also blessed each other. I had learned of an American Indian tradition called smudging, which can be done with a burning stick of dried sage or other aromatic herb, or with a feather. The feather is first used in downward strokes to brush the aura or energy field of the person being blessed. Then the feather is waved in an upward circular motion to balance the energy centers or chakras.

We began using these feather blessings at that first ceremony. Whenever anyone entered the work space to help us paint, they would first be blessed in order to honor them for being there and as a way of making the space seem sacred and different from the world outside.

We had another blessing ceremony at the opening of our first public walk that included a feather blessing for all who were present. Here is the blessing that was offered by the Rev. Susan Power Trucksess on that evening.

To speak of the labyrinth and its possibilities is to try to put words around a mystery, or more accurately, a number of mysteries.

To say it is one thing and not another, risks misconstruing, misleading, or limiting the experience.

It might be safe to talk in terms or images of celebration, rebirth, journeying, illumination, transformation.

All of these processes I mentioned involve movement and change. But we must be careful not to assume that that means they move in a linear fashion—going from here to there, in a forward-only direction.

So let us consider what growth, transformation, change, which are universal experiences, might look like . . . depending on your perspective.

The biologist observes the butterfly emerge from the cocoon and calls it "transformation."

The psychologist watches for shedding of old patterns and development of new ones in the various stages of life—and proclaims "transformation."

The Old Testament gives the promise of the crocus blooming in the desert and the lion lying down with the lamb—and declares "transformation."

The Christian knows of rebirth, and conversion, and reorientation, and calls these "transformation."

Some are more comfortable describing this process as a return to the center which was once known but has been forgotten.

I cannot tell you, I cannot even imagine, what you might experience tonight.

I only know that three months ago what we have here on the floor of this sanctuary tonight existed as canvas, paint, and individuals who were willing to labor on a project that was only a vision, only a possibility.

And tonight we have our own labyrinth and folks who have already experienced its powers.

Who knows what will be possible for you as you travel its pathway? May you encounter blessings.

Who knows with what you will connect? May blessings abound.

Who knows what transformation and illumination may occur?

May your movements and insights be blessed.

Let us pray before the awesomeness of such a mystery.

I have collected here a sample blessing ceremony for each of the days of the year when we offer our walks in Connecticut. These include the solstices and the equinoxes, the cross-quarter days that fall directly between them, and several other holidays that are fun to celebrate. They fall roughly once a month, skipping January and July, which we have always omitted.

One of the great joys of this work has been the fun of using rituals, prayers, and blessings from many different traditions, often within one ceremony. You are welcome to use, adapt, or mix and match any of the following versions to meet your own particular needs or special occasions. Among many wonderful sources, we are fond of using *Earth Prayers* by Elizabeth Roberts and Elias Amidon, Nigel Pennick's *The Pagan Book of Days*, and Danaan Parry's *The Essene Book of Days* as resources. However, any sacred texts or prayers can be used along with readings from your own spiritual tradition. We feel that this is ecumenism at its very best.

I usually invite one of our board members to work on each ceremony with me. Sometimes we do all of the readings ourselves. Sometimes we invite the participants to do some of them too, just handing them out randomly to strangers as they arrive. We love the spontaneity of this and people like being asked to be involved.

Over the years we have developed a format for our blessings that has remained the same. Except in the warmest summer months, we use votive candles around the labyrinths and often set up altars in the four directions or use other decorations depending on the season. I always start by walking down the aisle and into the center of the big labyrinth, where I turn to face the participants who are seated in rows at the back of the church. I begin by ringing the Ting Sha, which is a Tibetan chime, but any bell or drum would also do.

When the sound has completely disappeared into the space, I welcome everyone, make any announcements, invite those who can walk without the support of their shoes to remove them, and ask that everyone join me in a circle on the labyrinth. When the blessing is finished, I declare that the labyrinths are now open and wish everyone Godspeed on their journey.

February

As we have always taken January off to recover from the holidays, February is our first walk of the year and it offers two days to choose from: the cross-quarter day of Imbolc or Candlemas on February 1, and Valentine's Day on February 14.

Blessing Ceremony for Imbolc or Candlemas

FEBURARY 1
(DESIGNED WITH ELAINE FOSTER)

EXPLANATION

Imbolc is the cross-quarter day that falls directly between the winter solstice and the spring equinox. It is said that this is the day that seeds first begin to grow and move under the earth and it is the time of the birthing of the first lambs. For the ancient peoples it was the first day of spring. In the Christian tradition it is the day of Candlemas, the feast of the purification of the Virgin Mary.

LITANY

(Leader) I am rooted firmly in the Earth.
(Participants) I know that I am blessed.

It is this grounded me that I honor this night.
I know that I am blessed.

For without this grounding there could be no expansion.
I know that I am blessed.

The earth is my home for this incarnation and
I know that I am blessed.

PRAYER

As in many spiritual traditions we ask for the blessings of the seven directions and we light a candle in honor of each of them. Beginning in the East, we ask for the blessings of the direction of the East, the place of new beginnings, inspiration, and sunrises. We ask for the blessings of the direction of the South, the place of passion, warmth, and enthusiasm. We ask for the blessings of the direction of the West, the place of intuition and inner knowing. We ask for the blessings of the direction of the North, the place of communication and community. We ask for the blessings of the direction below and we take a moment to send our loving energy deep into our mother Earth. We ask for the blessings of the direction above and remember that we are connected to all there is all the way to the edges of the universe and beyond. We ask for the blessings of the direction within as that is the direction that our labyrinth journey will take us.

Great Spirit, we ask for the awareness of your presence here with us now in this place, that the pathways of the labyrinths will be filled with your divine light and love, and that the centers will be truly a place of enlightenment for each of us. We ask your blessings on each of us gathered here and on those who are yet to come, and we honor the Virgin Mary on this her day of purification. Amen.

The labyrinths are open. We wish you Godspeed on your journey. Blessed be.

Blessing Ceremony for Valentine's Day

FEBRUARY 14
(DESIGNED WITH MARY LOUISE COX)

EXPLANATION

St. Valentine's day is a festival of love that amalgamates the Pagan traditions of Rome and northern Europe. It is also dedicated to the Norse deity Vali, the archer god, son of Odin, and to Juno Februa, goddess of love. The festival begins after sunset on February 13. Girls should decorate their pillows with five bay leaves, to dream of their lover and husband-to-be. In England on this day an arch of brambles is carried to banish unwelcome spirits. In Scandinavia there is a tradition of running labyrinths on this day.

—*The Essene Book of Days*

BLESSING

As in many ancient traditions around the world, we are going to honor the four directions for their special powers to inform our understanding of the various aspects of love and light a candle for each one.

Beginning in the East, the place of inspiration and sunrises:

A reading from *The Essene Book of Days* by Danaan Parry—Tuesday, March 3:

How strong in me is my need to grow, to expand to meet the promise of the coming spring. There is a joy in me that carries me onward from this physical being to the awareness of the cosmic ocean of Love in which I dwell. May I be blessed to share this joy with all beings, in whatever way I can.

And from the South, place of fire, passion and enthusiasm:

How do I love thee? Let me count the ways.
I love thee to the depth and breadth and height
My soul can reach, when feeling out of sight
For the ends of Being and ideal Grace.
—Elizabeth Barrett Browning

And from the West, the place of intuition:

About me flow the waters of nourishment;
Within me flows the water of nourishment.
My bloodstream is aglow with the impulse of life
As I challenge the dark places in my being,
As I expand beyond the security of the womb,
As I move past my own definitions.
And surrounding this, engulfing me,
Is the cosmic ocean of Love and Light
From whence I truly came.
—The Essene Book of Days

And finally, from the North, the place of community:

Someday after mastering the winds, the waves, the tides and gravity, we will harness for God the energies of love. And then, for the second time in the history of the world, men will have discovered fire.

—Teilhard de Chardin

PRAYER

Great Spirit, Mother Father God, Creator of all there is, we ask for the awareness of your presence here with us now in this place, that the pathways of the labyrinths be filled with your divine light and love, that the centers be truly a place of enlightenment and that each of us gathered here and those who are yet to come be blessed on every step of our journeys. Amen.

The labyrinths are open. We wish you Godspeed on your journey. Blessed be.

Blessing Ceremony for Spring Equinox

MARCH 21

EXPLANATION

Today we celebrate the vernal equinox, the spring equinox—the day exactly halfway between the solstices, the day that the sun shines directly on the equator and night and day are of equal length. It is Earth's day of balance—the only day when we can balance eggs on the table. Stand completely still for a moment and feel that balance.

Today also marks the end of the astrological year, the last day of Pisces. So tomorrow is the first day of Aries, the first day of spring, and the first day in a new year of the zodiac. We stand in celebration of the arrival of spring and the warmth of a new season.

PRAYER

We stand now in anticipation, asking the Divine Spirit of the Universe to bless each of us here and those who are yet to come, to fill the pathways of the labyrinths with divine light and love for all who will walk them this night.

We stand in expectation of the dawning of a New Age.

MEDITATION

And then all that has divided us will merge
And then compassion will be wedded to power
And then softness will come to a world that is harsh and unkind
And then both men and women will be gentle
And then both women and men will be strong
And then no person will be subject to another's will
And then all will be rich and free and varied
And then the greed of some will give way to the needs of many
And then all will share equally in the Earth's abundance
And then all will care for sick and the weak and the old
And then all will nourish the young
And then all will cherish life's creatures
And then all will live in harmony with each other and the Earth
And then everywhere will be called Eden once again.
—Judy Chicago

The labyrinths are open. We wish you Godspeed on your journey. Blessed be.

Blessing Ceremony for Easter Eve

(DESIGNED WITH ELAINE FOSTER)

EXPLANATION

The intention of this blessing ceremony is to celebrate renewal, rebirth, free-dom, enlightenment, immortality, and so I ask you to join with me in asking the Holy Spirit to be present here tonight in this space, with all of us gathered here, and with those who are yet to come, and especially to be present on the pathways of the labyrinth, so that all who walk will feel the divine presence of the Holy One. I light this candle in honor of the Creator—may its flame glow within each of us. Amen

After the final blessing you are each invited to light your candle from the center candle and to place it anywhere around the outer edge of the canvas.

As we gather on the road to Easter, between the darkness of death and the dawn of resurrection, we can follow the way of the cross, shedding the old consciousness so that the spirit of the new may enter and prepare us for the awakening.

PRAYER

Let us be together in prayer.

> *Lord of wondrous patience, the earth has risen again, emerging from a darkness in a way it*
> *has never quite been before; Whirling to a fresh time, an unused space:*
> *Alive with trembling possibilities, and I with it! Such staggering grace!*

Please, nurture me in newness; set me free from the tyrannies of habit and complaining and blaming;

Shake from me the dusty melancholy of too much success and comfort, pride and pretense, that, as if on the first day of creation, we may begin to see the miracle of life and humanity;

To hear the hum of grace unfolding to meet all my needs, unexpectedly and surprisingly, and urging me to go in faith to whatever is next in love. Amen.

—Ted Loder
<small>GUERRILLAS OF GRACE</small>

The labyrinths are open. We wish you Godspeed on your journey. Blessed be.

Blessing Ceremony for Earth Day

APRIL 22
(DESIGNED WITH ESTHER BRODIE)

EXPLANATION

The Earth is our Mother, whatever befalls the earth befalls the sons and daughters of the Earth. The Earth does not belong to us, we belong to the Earth, this we know. All things are connected. The Earth will take care of us, if we will take care of the Earth.

—Chief Seattle

As we pass the ball representing the earth around the circle, I invite you to hold it tenderly for a moment and offer to the earth a prayer of gratitude and a prayer for peace.

BLESSING

The following is a reading from *Earth Prayers:*

> *O our Mother the Earth, blessed is your name.*
> *Blessed are your fields and forests, your rocks and mountains, your grasses and trees and flowers, and every green and growing thing.*
> *Blessed are your streams and lakes and rivers, the oceans where our life began, and all your waters that sustain our bodies and refresh our souls.*
> *Blessed is the air we breathe, your atmosphere, that surrounds us and binds us to every living thing.*
> *Blessed are all creatures who walk along your surface or swim in your waters or fly through your air, for they are all our relatives.*
> *Blessed are all people who share this planet, for we are all one family, and the same spirit moves through us all . . .*
> *O Great Spirit whose voice we hear in the wind and whose face we see in the morning sun, blessed is your name.*
> *Help us to remember that you are everywhere and teach us the way of peace.*
> —Helen Weaver

PRAYER

From the Hebrew tradition:

> *Barukh attah Adonai Eloheinu Melekh ha-Olam, she-heheyanu v'kiy'manu v'higi'anu la-z'man ha-zeh.*
> *"Praised art Thou, Lord our God, King of the Universe, for granting us life, for sustaining us, and for helping us to reach this day."*

I would like to acknowledge the blessings that we receive each day from each of the four elements: the air that we breathe, the fire that warms us, the water that restores and cleanses us, and the earth that supports our lives.

Let us take a moment now to speak out loud a word of gratitude for the Earth. *(Everyone around the circle speaks a word, such as flowers, rainbows, sunshine, etc.)*

Great Spirit, Mother Father God, we ask for the awareness of your presence here with us now in this place, that the pathways of the labyrinths be filled with your divine light and love, that the center be truly a place of enlightenment for each of us. We ask blessings on those of us who are gathered here and on those who are yet to come and ask that all of our collective prayers and meditations will finally bring peace to everyone, all across the whole Earth. Amen.

The labyrinths are open. I wish you Godspeed on your journey. Blessed be.

Blessing for May Day

MAY 1

EXPLANATION
Our blessing ceremony this evening is inspired by the *Essene Book of Days,* and so it connects us back to the pre-Christian Community of the Essenes. Half

of Jesus's twelve disciples were Essenes, including his most important teacher, John the Baptist. It is the Essenes who are thought to have written the Dead Sea Scrolls.

And so we come to May Day.

Reading from "Introduction to Beltane" from the *Essene Book of Days* by Danaan Parry:

> *The first day of May has been celebrated for thousands of years as the point of fertility, as a time when nature blatantly displays its beauty to bring about the conception of new life. In Celtic tradition, it is known as Beltane . . . or the magic of flowers . . .*
> *We are here upon this earth for a purpose, and a major aspect of this is to be of authentic service, to share our light and our love genuinely as we grow in consciousness.*
> *This is a time of doing, of making love manifest on the physical plane . . .*

The phrase *making love manifest* feels to me like a call to action, an invitation, a challenge, if you will. How many ways are there to make love manifest on the physical plane? I invite each of you now to stand in silence for a moment and to call forth from within yourselves all of the ways in which you can make love manifest in your lives.

PRAYER

And now let us pray. Great Spirit God, Creator of all there is, we ask your presence with us now in this place, that the pathways of the labyrinths be filled with your divine light and love, that the center be for each of us truly a place of enlightenment, and that throughout our journeys, we feel your presence with us, guiding us, and showing us how to make love manifest each step along the way. Amen.

BLESSING

I invite you to pass this blessing around the circle. Placing your hand on their heart chakra, say to the person on your right, *I honor the God in you. Make love manifest in the world.*

The labyrinths are open. I wish you Godspeed on your journey. Blessed be.

Blessing Ceremony for Summer Solstice

JUNE 21
(DESIGNED WITH LOIS HOROWITZ)

EXPLANATION

Sunrise on the day of the summer solstice has been honored by the peoples of the earth for thousands of years. Literally, it is the day Earth changes the axis on which it rotates so that the Northern Hemisphere now leans more toward the sun than the Southern Hemisphere does.

To Mayans, Aztecs, ancient Scandinavians, Egyptians, Celts, some Native Americans, and some Christian religions, it was also a day of symbolic ceremony for the infusion of light from its greatest source in the material world—the sun. Like those who have come before us, we gather here today to infuse ourselves and these labyrinths with our own ceremony of light, and to make a connection with those in other time zones around the planet who have either already done or are about to do a similar ceremony, which will eventually encircle the earth.

Some of you may not be aware that this eleven-circuit labyrinth is a replica of the Chartres Cathedral labyrinth in France, and that the only day of the year it is cleared of chairs for a public walk is the summer solstice. So let us keep our parent labyrinth, and all who walk it, in mind during our ceremony tonight.

BLESSING

Begin with your eyes closed, and take seven breaths to relax the body, calm the mind and attune ourselves to each other.

Visualize a large, radiant globe of light in the center of our circle.

Now imagine that you are able to draw a ray of light from the center globe and allow it to shower all aspects of your being with light.

Now allow that ray of light to extend beyond your body so that it connects with everyone else's ray and makes a complete circle around the labyrinth.

Now let that circle of light expand to include the seven-circuit labyrinth in the far corner.

Now as a form of blessing for the labyrinths and all who will walk them tonight, direct the light along the pathways of the labyrinths.

Now extend the light that we have created with our intent and allow it to fill the entire church all the way around and all the way up to the highest point on the ceiling.

Now allow the light to expand beyond the walls of the church and let it encompass the whole community, the entire State of Connecticut, and the whole country.

Now let the light grow so that the light that we have created merges with the light that has been created by all of the other solstice gatherings all across the other time zones and all the way around the earth.

Know that this light now encircles the earth and that it will be added to as the sun rises around the planet.

Now stand in your own fullness.

The labyrinths are open. We wish you Godspeed on your journey. Blessed be.

Blessing Ceremony for Lammas

AUGUST 1
(DESIGNED WITH WENDY BERRY AND ELAINE FOSTER)

EXPLANATION

Lammas is an Old English word meaning "Loaf Mass." It is an ancient Celtic festival celebrating the first harvest of the year, especially the first ripened grain of the growing season

Today, country fairs with their competitions for the biggest and best vegetables, are descendants of the age-old celebration of the wealth and bounty of the earth. This is the time of the year when Native Americans celebrate the Green Corn Ceremony, giving thanks when their first ears of corn are ripe enough to harvest. Among the Hopi, who use corn pollen and corn meal extensively in their rituals, the Mother Goddess is represented by a perfect ear of corn.

In the Celtic tradition, divinity was also symbolized by ripened grains. The

Celts believed that the sacred energy in a field of grain retreated as the grain was cut, concentrating its power into the grain that was still standing. For this reason, the last bundle of grain was believed to contain the spirit of the entire field. It was gathered up, tied around the middle with cloth or ribbon, and called the Grain Mother. Variations of this name, such as Corn Mother, Barley Mother, Wheat Mother, or Harvest Mother, were also used depending on the locality and what was grown there. The Grain Mother would be ceremoniously carried to the village and kept until the following spring, when her sacred seeds would be used to plant the next year's crop, to insure another successful harvest.

We can see in these ancient rituals the symbolic essence of the rhythms of nature, upon which we all depend. We can celebrate the ancient ways, and draw upon their power.

Whether or not we have soil to work with, we are all gardeners. We all plant seeds—the seeds of our dreams and goals and aspirations. We plant these seeds in the rich soil of our creativity. Like careful farmers, we tend our crop with patience and perseverance. We pull the weeds of disappointment, frustration, doubt, self-criticism, anger, and fear. Eventually our seeds will grow and flourish, and we will gather a plentiful harvest. What do you hope to harvest in your life?

At the close of this blessing ceremony I will hold a bowl of seeds. Each of you who wishes may take one to hold in your hand or to keep in your pocket to remind you during your walk of that which you are choosing to plant and to harvest in your life.

And now I invite you, in the words of Julian of Norwich (read from *Earth Prayers*):

BLESSING

(To) be a gardener. Dig a ditch, toil and sweat, and turn the earth upside down and seek the deepness and water the plants in time. Continue this labor and make sweet floods to run and noble and abundant fruits to spring. Take this food and drink and carry it to God as your true worship.

And so you may consider the three-part journey of your labyrinth walk this evening to be a harvest; the way into the center as the time of preparation and of planting; the time in the center as the time of germination and nurturing; and the time on the way back out as the harvest.

PRAYER

And so we ask now that the divine presence of the Creator of all that is be here with us now in this place, that the pathways of the labyrinths be filled with divine light and love and that the center be for each of us truly a place where we can harvest whatever is for our highest good.

Labyrinths are for all seasons. Walk with us tonight and celebrate your plantings and your reapings. Amen.

And so the labyrinths are open. We wish you Godspeed on your journey. Blessed be.

Blessing Ceremony for Fall Equinox

SEPTEMBER 21
(DESIGNED WITH CATHIE LeVASSEUR)

EXPLANATION

A reading on the autumn equinox from the *Essene Book of Days*:

This is the point on the wheel of the year when there is a balance between the energies of outward, physical, yang manifestation and inward, psychic, yin creativity. There [are] equal hours of daylight and darkness . . . [at this time as symbolized by our half circle of lighted candles.]

This balance point of the rational and the intuitive will exist for a moment, and then the forces of the intuitive, dark, inner contemplations will slowly ascend and rule the seasonal wheel through the winter. At Winter Solstice, the inner world of yin will be at its zenith.

We now enter the all-important time of inner growth. During summer, there was little time for the juices of contemplative creativity to bubble up from deep within us. Now is the time to prepare for this to occur most fruitfully. Only when we surrender to our inner nature can we begin to hear the still small voice within, and we must set our outer affairs in order now to be ready when it calls.

And so I invite you now to consider what is out of order or out of balance in your life that you are now ready to address in preparation for hearing that still small voice within. Pause for a moment in the silence to consider what you must do to regain your balance. What is it that you need to take on or let go of to set your affairs in order?

To help us bring the image of balance into our lives, we are going to celebrate a water ritual. We will bless each other with water, and as we pass the water around the circle, I invite you to notice how it always finds its own balance. Recall how it has been used down through the ages as an element of cleansing and purification. Allow yourself to feel blessed by it and to experience the balance between giving and receiving.

BLESSING

(Take two small pitchers, one empty and one filled with water. Hand the empty one to the person on your left. In silence slowly fill their pitcher with water. Then hand your now empty pitcher to the next person to the left. The person holding the now full pitcher turns and pours the water into the empty pitcher being held by the person on their left. They hand the now empty pitcher to the next person on the left. And so it goes around the circle with each person experiencing the receiving and the giving of the water. If the circle is large, two pairs of pitchers may be used, one pair poured to the left and one pair to the right so that they will meet at the opposite side of the circle.)

PRAYER

We pray that the pathways of the labyrinths be aligned with light and love, that all who walk on this journey may know the essence of balance.

The labyrinths are open. We wish you Godspeed on your journey. Blessed be.

Blessing Ceremony for the Harvest Time

(DESIGNED WITH ANNE HUSSEY)

EXPLANATION

This is the season when the harvest is gathered and we give thanks.

The following passages are from *Selu: Seeking the Corn-Mother's Wisdom* by Marilou Awiakta:

(Drum beat)

In the beginning, the Creator made our Mother Earth. Then came Selu, Grandmother Corn . . .

Sniffing the air, we seek the source—and find it. The cornfield in bloom. Row on row of sturdy stalks, with tassels held up to the moon. Silently, in slow rhythm, we make our way into the field. The faint rustle of growing plants flows around and through us, until, when we stop by a tall stalk, there seems no division between flesh and green. We rub the smooth, sinewy leaves on our checks and touch the nubile ear, where each grain of pollen that falls from the tassel will make a kernel, strong and turgid with milk. Linking arms around the stalk, we lift our faces to the drifting pollen and breathe the spirit of the Corn-Mother—the powerful, joyous, nurturing odor of one complete-in-herself.

In the faraway times of which we are speaking, the People acknowledged this source. And they came to know corn . . . in the senses: mother, enabler, transformer, healer. From time immemorial, whenever the People have migrated, in the Four Directions, they have taken Grandmother Corn with them, passing the whole corn—the grain and its story, its sacred meaning—from generation to generation.

BLESSING

All say in unison: We ask for the blessing of the spirit of each of the four directions to be with us on the labyrinths. Spirit of the North, Mother, the power of Earth. Spirit of the East, Enabler, the power of Air. Spirit of the South, Transformer, the power of Fire. Spirit of the West, Healer, the power of Water.

Again, from *Selu:*

> *Wherever I journeyed in the Four Directions, people listened to the traditional story . . . "The corn is like our people. It draws strength from its clan. A single stalk will bear nothing." Always take your heritage with you. "And be like the seed. Protect your life. Live deep in your spirit until the time to come forth." . . . When I held up an ear of calico corn, we would think together about this wisdom of the Corn-Mother. How different colored kernels are ranged around the cob, no one more important than the other. How each kernel respects the space of those on either side, yet remains itself—red, black, white, yellow, or combinations of those colors. How the Corn-Mother, in her physical being, exemplifies unity in diversity.*

All say in unison: May the Great Spirit of the Universe be present on the labyrinths for each of us—red, black, white, yellow, or combinations of those colors.

From *Selu:*

> *The seeds of one decade are the harvest of the next.*
>
> *I offer you something so small that my thumb and forefinger almost cover it. It's a communication that's faster than fax, more personal than poetry and more ancient than words. When you hold out your hand, I lay a corn seed in your palm. A symbol of hope.*

In the split second the shell first touched your skin, the tip of my finger touched you also. Energy to energy, life to life, and invitation to a journey . . .

I wish you Godspeed on your journey. Amen.
(Circle dance around and off the labyrinth to the drum beat.)

Blessing Ceremony for All Saints' Day

NOVEMBER 1
(DESIGNED WITH MARY LOUISE COX)

EXPLANATION
At this time of the year when the seeds fall to the earth to be reborn again in the spring, we celebrate the Circle of Life as we honor those who are dear to us who have gone on to be reborn into new life.

I invite all of you to share in this reading from Ecclesiastes. We will pass it around and each of us will read a phrase.

To everything there is a season,
And a time to every purpose under heaven:
A time to be born,
And a time to die;
A time to plant,

And a time to pluck up that which was planted;
A time to kill,
And a time to heal;
A time to break down,
And a time to build up;
A time to weep,
And a time to laugh;
A time to mourn,
And a time to dance;
A time to cast away stones,
And a time to gather stones together;
A time to embrace,
And a time to refrain from embracing;
A time to seek,
And a time to lose;
A time to keep,
And a time to cast away;
A time to rend,
And a time to sew;
A time to keep silent,
And a time to speak;
A time to love,
And a time to hate;
A time for war,
And a time for peace.

Before you sit down to prepare for your labyrinth walk, I invite you to take a slip of paper from one of the pedestals and write down the names of the saints in your lives who have gone on before you and who you wish to honor and hold with you as you walk this night. Our blessing of the labyrinths this evening will open and close with prayers from the Hindu tradition. Let us pray.

PRAYER

> *O thou shining one,*
> *Thou knowest all our ways,*
> *We utter praise of thee!*
> *Thou art woman, thou art man;*
> *Thou art youth, thou art maiden . . .*
> *Thou art the dark blue bee,*
> *Thou art the green parrot with the red eyes,*
> *Thou art the thunder cloud,*
> *The seasons, the seas.*
> *Thou art our Father, Thou art our Mother,*
> *Thou art our Beloved Friend.*

We ask your presence here with us now in this place, that the pathways of the labyrinths be filled with your light and love, that each of us gathered here and those who are yet to come, be filled with your blessings.

> *From the unreal lead us to the real;*
> *From the darkness lead us to the light;*
> *From death lead us to deathlessness.*
> *Amen.*

The labyrinths are open. We wish you Godspeed on your journey. Blessed be.

Blessing Ceremony for Winter Solstice

DECEMBER 21
(DESIGNED WITH ELAINE FOSTER)

EXPLANATION

Welcome to this evening's labyrinth walk in celebration of the winter solstice, the midnight of the year. Take a moment to notice the candles that make a complete circle around the labyrinths, and see that there are plastic lighters for you to use to light the candles at the close of this blessing. I invite you to light them in honor of whatever you wish to light up in your life.

Our ritual this evening is in the form of a litany. We will conclude each reading by saying in unison the words "May the darkness illuminate the light." Then there will be a moment of silence, followed by the ringing of the Ting Sha. We ask that each of the readers wait to begin reading until after the sound of the Ting Sha has faded away. The readings will be accompanied by the lowering of the electric lights until we are standing still and silent in complete darkness.

LITANY

Twilight is a time for sharing—and a time for remembering—the shadows of the gathering dusk—Here our two worlds meet and pass—the frantic sounds of man grow dimmer as the light recedes—the unhurried rhythm of the other world swells in volume as the darkness deepens. Memories burn more brightly—as the things of substance lose their line and form in the softness of the dark. Listen tonight with all with wisdom of your spirit—listen too with all the compassion of your heart.

—Winston Abbot, "Blessed be the Night"
from EARTH PRAYERS

(Participants) *"May the darkness illuminate the light"* (Silence, Ting Sha)

Great Spirit God, Creator of Darkness, be with each of us who walk these labyrinths this night. That their paths may guide and protect us on our way as we attain the center and search for the truth.

"May the darkness illuminate the light" (Silence, Ting Sha)

There is in God, some say, a deep but dazzling darkness.

—Henry Vaughan

"May the darkness illuminate the light" (Silence, Ting Sha)

(Total darkness, sound of long, low cello; the candles are lit.)

The labyrinths are open. We wish you Godspeed on your journey. Blessed be.

Blessing Ceremony for New Year's Eve

DECEMBER 31
(DESIGNED WITH HELEN CITRIN)

EXPLANATION

Welcome to this New Year's Eve labyrinth walk. You will notice that we have a burning bowl available so that you may write down anything that you no longer wish to carry with you into the new year. Then just touch the corner of the paper to the candle flame and drop the burning paper into the bowl.

Our New Year's Eve Blessing Ceremony tonight is dedicated to peace and we will end it with a Sacred Circle Dance. Sacred Circle Dancing is used in many cultures as an expression of prayer. It is said that if you speak your prayer, you pray once. If you sing your prayer, you pray twice, and if you dance your prayer, you pray three times.

MEDITATION

The most powerful point in any cycle is its birthing point. The initiatory thrust of a new beginning is always charged with hope and promise.

—Ken Kalb

Let us make that hope and that promise be one of peace as we stand on the threshold of a whole new year.

In order for the world to become peaceful, people must become peaceful. Among mature people war would not be a problem—it would be impossible. . . . The sanctuary of peace dwells within. Seek it out and all things will be added to you. We are coming closer and closer to the time when enough of us will have found inner peace. And the shift that will change the world is one of higher consciousness—an opening, a potential opportunity for each person to receive their full self.

—PEACE PILGRIM: HER LIFE AND WORK IN HER OWN WORDS

PRAYER

Great Spirit, Loving God, grant us thy peace. We ask for the awareness of your divine presence here with us now in this place, that the pathways of the labyrinths may be filled with light and love, that the new year comes for each of us whenever it is that we reach the center, that each of us gathered here and those who are yet to come will be blessed every step of our journeys. Amen.

MEDITATION

(To be said in unison, from the *Essene Book of Days* [Dec. 31] by Parry.)

As the clear winter water nourishes the seed within the earth, I am nourished by new-found awareness of who I truly am. This awareness has not yet fully matured, and I rest content in the arms of the unfolding universe, which will reveal all wisdom in its time. The Power of the unmanifest even now works within my spiritual heart and I am at peace.

(Circle Dance around and off the labyrinth.)

The labyrinths are open. I wish you Godspeed on your journey. Blessed be.

Closing Ceremonies

While we have not traditionally had closing ceremonies at our public labyrinth walks, I almost always do them at my workshops. Many of the elements included in the Blessing Ceremonies could be adapted and used for a closing—for example, the blowing out of a candle instead of the lighting of one. The passing of the water blessing, the burning bowl, or a Sacred Circle Dance would all also work well for a closing.

There is a blessing that can be passed from one person to another around a circle in which I turn to the person on my right and place my right hand on their heart chakra. Then they ask me, "Who is this person who stands before me?" I respond, "I am you, just in another form." They turn and place their right hand on the person to their right, who asks them the same question: "Who is this who stands before me?" They answer, "I am you, just in another form," and so it goes around the circle.

It is my hope that these sample ceremonies will provide you with a rich base of material on which to design your own. We all love ceremony and ritual in one way or another, and all labyrinths need to be blessed. You don't need anyone else's permission or approval to create the perfect blessing ceremony for your needs. All you need is to trust that all will be for the highest good, and it will be. Blessed be.

CHAPTER 11

Creating and Sharing Labyrinths

I love giving labyrinth workshops because they can help people gain more knowledge and a deeper appreciation of labyrinths. Since we spend a day—rather than an hour—walking and focusing on the labyrinth experience, there is more opportunity for insights during a workshop than there might be at a public walk. Labyrinth workshops bring people together in a special way. Many workshops are set up with a specific agenda or intention for the group to work on. For example, I have done workshops with countless church groups trying to strengthen their sense of connection with their faith.

In all my labyrinth workshops, I start with basics: an explanation of what a labyrinth is, the history of labyrinths, the materials they have been made of, how they have been used over time, and how they are used today. I usually try to get everyone onto the labyrinth and walking early in the workshop. Doing so helps them see, first-hand, what we're talking about. I include cleansing and blessing ceremonies before the walks. Afterward, everyone shares their stories of what came up during the walk.

For groups working with a specific intention, I make modifications, such as helping them acknowledge and focus upon the intention. If the group comes from a particular religious or cultural tradition, the blessing ties into their tradition.

After the discussion, we do a hands-on activity, such as learning to draw the three-circuit and seven-circuit labyrinths. If there is time, and the group is working toward a shared goal, we walk the labyrinth again. This time, the emphasis is on team building; I ask the participants to become aware of the others in the group who are on the labyrinth, how the group as a whole moves through the walk, and the energy of the group. Then we gather for another discussion, specifically focusing on the group and its intentions.

Timelines and the Labyrinth

One of the most valuable exercises for me at the first labyrinth workshop I attended (given by Lauren Artress) was writing a timeline of my life. You begin by ticking off your life's important events. Note the passages, people entering and leaving, and milestones. After I did my timeline, I experienced instant shifts as I made the turns on the labyrinth; at one point, I suddenly found I was back in time to the day my father died.

The timeline is useful for group workshops as well. I ask participants to

It was beautiful when we stood together in the final circle. I was surprised at what people came up with as their single word meditations. Light. Joy. Meditation. Unity. Peace. Tranquility. Serenity. Thank you. I think this will make a big difference to our congregation.
—BOOK OF REFLECTIONS

write a timeline of their interactions and relationships with the particular group. If, for example, you've been a volunteer of an organization, then became a full-time employee, you might reflect on the entire time you've been a part of that particular community. You might recall milestones and memorable moments with the group. You might acknowledge what you like or dislike, together with what changes you think are needed.

The exercise offers an opportunity for participants to view their personal history in the context of their relationship to the group. You can reflect on what you know of the history of the group, whether you're a relative newcomer, or one of the founders. Looking at the personal relationship between each participant and the group as a whole, people often uncover insights, such as discovering that their personal needs have been translated into expectations for the group.

Children on the Labyrinth

> *Our family walk brings us closer together— each year, each walk, each step.*
>
> —BOOK OF REFLECTIONS

We have always welcomed children at our public walks, if they can be quiet. Although some children will run directly across the paths to the center, others seem to understand intuitively what this is all about even without being told. My advice to families with small children is by all means bring them with you to a labyrinth walk, provided that you think they will not disturb the other walkers. I know that this can be open to interpretation. Following one walk that we had a number of years ago, we had comments that the children were too loud and disruptive, while another person loved their energy and thought having the children was wonderful.

This dilemma was the impetus that led Cathie LeVasseur, board member of the Labyrinth Project of Connecticut and mother of one of the noisy kids that evening, to create our first Family Walk specifically for families with young children. These have become a tradition that we continue to offer from time to time. At these "Kids' Walks" we don't even try to keep it quiet. We play upbeat music, Cathie and her husband Paul give a brief introduction for the children, and we always have plenty of art supplies on hand for creative expressions. We let everyone run around all over the place: babies crawl, toddlers toddle, big kids show off or try to get to the center first. Moms and dads walk hand in hand with kids on hips, and kids show the way, leading their parents and tugging them forward to the center or back out.

Unless you are attending this type of walk, prepare your children for a regular public labyrinth walk the same way you would prepare them for going to

Kids during a Family Walk.

a church or temple service. Explain that some things will be the same as being in church. People will want them to be quiet so they don't interrupt their meditations or prayers. There may be soft music, and it may not be a good place to ask lots of questions out loud. You can reassure them that you will answer their questions on the way home, so they should try to remember what they want to tell you for later, the way they would a dream or a movie.

I'd also explain the differences between a church service and labyrinth walk: people won't be sitting still. They will need to take off their shoes and they will walk along a path without bumping into anyone else. You can challenge them to see how quietly they can walk.

If your child finishes the walk before you do, tell them to find a place to sit down. Bring a book, something to draw on, or a favorite stuffed animal to occupy them until you finish your walk. That way Mom or Dad has a chance for at least part of a peaceful walk. Remember that children pick up their parents' vibrations with the most sensitive antennae. The degree to which you are open and comfortable with walking the labyrinth will influence your child's experience.

Creating Your Own Full-Size Labyrinths

There is something so special about being able to walk a full-size labyrinth, you may find yourself wishing you had one of your own. While creating a labyrinth has its challenges, it is not impossible. You may not have a field in which you can mow a labyrinth, or a garden or yard with enough space. Even so, you can create your own labyrinth.

The portable labyrinths used by the Labyrinth Project of Connecticut for public walks are made from duck, which is a very thick canvas. They are large and heavy, and are each constructed in two or three sections to accommodate storage and travel. For public walks, such durable, industrial-strength canvas is crucial. To create a portable labyrinth for your own use does not require you to go to such lengths. All you need is a flat white king-size bed sheet to make a wonderful personal portable labyrinth.

Use the seed pattern from page 113 to draw the seven-circuit labyrinth onto the sheet. Color the "walls" as the Connecticut Project did. As an alternative to coloring the walls, you could color the paths. (Experiment with different kinds of paint depending on whether you want it to be washable or not.) Suddenly you have a labyrinth you can walk anywhere there's space to lay out the sheet. In addition to walking, you can sleep under the labyrinth. Imprint the labyrinth on your dreams!

Drawing the Eleven-Circuit Chartres Labyrinth

Unlike drawing the classical labyrinths from seed patterns as you have just learned to do, drawing the eleven-circuit Chartres labyrinth is no simple or easy matter. Fortunately, now it is no longer necessary to draw them yourself if you don't want to. There are several sources for ready-made canvas Chartres labyrinths listed in the Recommended Resources section of this book. Back in 1993 when we started the Labyrinth Project of Connecticut, however, this was not the case.

Ours was only the second or third canvas labyrinth ever to be made, according to Lauren Artress. With an early draft of her seed kit, which hadn't even been printed yet, and the steady hand of industrial designer and now Connecticut Project board member Stephen Fog, somehow we managed to get the design onto the canvas. We documented the whole process in our wonderful 27-minute video called *Walking in Sacred Circles,* which is still available.

Since that time I have created another one on canvas for the Community Labyrinth of Pelham, New York, and I have also done them outdoors.

LESSONS FROM THE LABYRINTH

In the summer of 1998, I traveled to Vilnius, Lithuania, with Judith Joyce, vice president of the Labyrinth Society, to facilitate a labyrinth workshop for psychologists and family therapists. We had to find some inexpensive lightweight material with which to create a temporary outdoor labyrinth for the conference. My daughter called from college with the answer. She told me her sorority sisters had just played a trick called "forking the lawn" on a fraternity house. It gave me the idea of using plastic forks stuck in the ground to create the labyrinth in Lithuania. So we brought bags and bags of plastic forks. They were lightweight and easy to pack. There would be no damage to the environment, and we sailed through customs!

However, the forks were clear plastic and we quickly learned that the minute we placed them into the ground and moved a few feet away, they appeared to be invisible. Both Judith and I were master labyrinth builders by anybody's standards at that time, but building this labyrinth became near to impossible for us. Every time we got one line in place we would move around to the next one and completely lose the first one. I don't know how we ever got it straightened out in time, but somehow we managed. The lessons from that labyrinth: plastic forks are great material for temporary labyrinths, buy at least double the number you think you'll need, and be sure they are a nice bright color!

Following is my attempt to explain the process to you so that you can get an idea of the scope of the project. It is not intended to be a substitute for the Veriditas seed kit or for the excellent instructional materials that have been produced by Robert Ferré of the St. Louis Labyrinth Project. Nor is it intended to teach you how to make anything close to an exact replica of the Chartres labyrinth. Again, I leave that to experts like Robert Ferré and master craftsman, Marty Kermeen of Artpavers, both of whom are fellow Labyrinth Society members.

Finally, remembering that, as labyrinth builder Alex Champion has said, "the most important thing about building a labyrinth is the prayers that go into it," here is what I do when making a Chartres labyrinth. For simplicity's sake lets suppose that this is going to be an outdoor labyrinth. I will let you know when things come up that are unique to drawing them on canvas.

1. Pray.

2. Locate and mark the center by driving a stake into the ground. I use the thin green bamboo stakes available at all garden centers because they are lightweight, cheap, and I can slip the end of my Stanley tape measure onto them. (This is essential.) When drawing on canvas, mark the center with an X made of masking tape and draw a dot on the tape.

3. Decide on the orientation of the entrance into the center using a compass or by dowsing or by sighting it on some fixed object and drive a stake into the ground to mark that direction (but well beyond the distance where the outer edge of the labyrinth will actually be). On canvas you will need to mark it with masking tape on the floor beyond the edge of the canvas. Then tie a string from the center stake to the entrance marker stake. Using masking tape if you are working on canvas. Note that we are creating the imaginary line that runs directly into the center of the labyrinth, not the line which is the center of the entrance path, as that is offset by one path-width to the left. Note: it is crucial when making a canvas labyrinth that the sections of the canvas be seamed together in such a way as to give you a center seam that runs straight up the middle of the labyrinth. All of your measurements are going to be taken off of this center seam, which you have now just covered with masking tape.

4. Repeat this process in the remaining four directions so that you have divided the area into four equal quadrants with perfect right angles at the center stake. I have always referred to the entrance of the labyrinth as 6:00 and the top as 12:00. Therefore, at this point you should have a string that runs from 6:00 past the center stake (but not tied to it) and directly up to 12:00, and another one that runs from 9:00 to 3:00. Mark these lines with ribbon on the stakes so they are clearly visible. In the case of a canvas labyrinth, the two axes are drawn on masking tape.

5. Now you need to place two more pairs of lines that run all the way across the labyrinth, one pair on each side of the horizontal axis to mark the width of the labrys or switchbacks at 9:00 and 3:00. Then, you need to do the same thing vertically at 12:00. It is important to decide how big these are going to be, particularly when drawing on canvas, so that you know where to stop drawing your circles. We quickly discovered there was no way to erase a pencil line once it had been drawn on the canvas. Robert Ferré has a motto: "If the line isn't right, don't draw it." We tried about a dozen different kinds of erasers with little or no success. It wasn't until after we had created our third labyrinth on canvas that our canvas supplier, The Norwalk Awning Company informed us that there was such a thing as a canvas eraser and we were welcome to pick one up whenever we needed it.

Outdoors I use red or orange spray paint for my markers and then I outline the paths with a white field marker that I borrow from the town soccer association. I always bring along a can of green spray paint so that I can "erase."

6. Now add two more strings, or lines of tape, to mark the path width at the entrance. Do the entrance path to the center first, by measuring one-half

path-width on either side of the center vertical axis. Then measure another path-width to the left of the center one to create the entrance at the mouth of the labyrinth, or 6:00.

7. Now it is time to begin to draw the circles. The center of the Chartres labyrinth is one quarter of the diameter of the entire labyrinth, which is slightly more than seven of the measurement units that are created by adding one path-width and one wall width. Remember that in making the circles, you are making the radius, which is one half of the diameter. Using a tape measure attached to the center post works well because it doesn't stretch the way rope does. When painting outdoors, mark the measurements of the circles directly on the tape measure with masking tape. In the case of canvas, measure out from the center and mark the size of the circles on the masking tape on the four axes. Measure the radius of the center and make the mark for your first circle. There are eleven more marks to make, each spaced apart by the same unit of one path and one wall.

   No matter what material you are using to build your wall, or how thick your line of paint is going to be, you will need to have determined it in advance in order for this to come out right.

8. Pray and take a deep breath.

9. Continue making your tick marks all the way out until you have twelve marks, the last of which marks the outside of the outer wall. The corona will be beyond that, but we will get to that later.

10. I do the same thing at each of the four quadrants so that when I am done I have four lines of tick marks as guidelines. Go ahead and make four more lines of marks that will divide each quadrant diagonally.

11. Now all you need to do is draw the circles to connect the tick marks. Here is where is helps to have a friend. While you are either pushing the line-marking machine across the grass or bending over with the pencil in your hand you will need to have your free hand holding the tape measure that is attached to the center stake. You will be using the tape measure as a compass to help you make perfect circle lines. While doing all of this it is nearly impossible to also be holding a drawing of the labyrinth and to keep in mind where you are on the big picture. Have your friend do this for you, shouting "stop" every time you come to a switchback so that you do not continue to draw that line past where it is supposed to be. If no friends are available, be sure to mark these places with another tick in advance so you will know when you come to them.

12. Pray and try to stand up.

13. Now you will need to fill in the rounded labrys semicircles. Robert uses a template for all of these.

14. Next you will need to complete the lines at the entrance.

15. In order to draw the six petals in the center, it is important to note that there are five little "crosses" where the petals intersect and two at the entrance that each have only one arm so that they don't protrude into the entrance path. They are left out of many contemporary versions of the Chartres labyrinth but they make drawing the center easier. The tips of these crosses are exactly halfway between the first circle and the center. The key to making the petal is to mark out the location of these crosses first, then draw the circles.

Three of these crosses are possible to locate immediately, the two on either side of the entrance and the one at 12:00. That leaves only two crosses on each side to locate. Knowing they are halfway out from the center and equidistant from each other, it is pretty easy to guesstimate where they should be. Spray a little dot on the ground or mark them on masking tape on canvas. Measure between the crosses and adjust them if necessary. Then draw the petals.

16. Finally, it is time to do the corona, which is second only to the center in its ability to challenge me. The greatest day of my labyrinth-building career was when I learned from Robert Ferré that even the original labyrinth in Chartres doesn't have completely even lunations all the way around the corona. There is a fudge factor.

    When painting outside, and just making "rays" for the corona, measure the diameter of the labyrinth and divide by 36. The rays are this distance apart. Make the first one at 12:00 and then draw around on each side from 12:00 to entrance. A yardstick comes in handy for spacing. You can also mark the length of the ray on the yardstick to keep them somewhat uniform. The length of the ray is the same as the distance between the rays. When you get five or six rays away from the entrance, measure ahead so you can see how much to fudge to make the distance between the last ray and the opening of the entrance equal to one half the distance between the rays.

    To make the corona on canvas, mark off the location of the ray by making small pencil marks on the canvas outside of the outer circle, in the area that will ultimately be painted. The first time around, separate your marks by a distance of $\frac{1}{36}$th of the diameter of the labyrinth. Going clockwise on the left side of the entrance, the first mark is one half of the spacing distance from the entrance path. Then continue to make your marks. When you get to the ray at 12:00, it should be ray number 56. If it isn't exactly right, measure the distance that you are off, either plus or minus, and divide this by 54. The answer may only be a quarter of an inch, or even less. Change your spacing accordingly and mark out the rays again. Now use this measurement for the right side beginning to the right of the entrance. Not counting the ray at 12:00, you should have 57 rays on the right side. Again, if you are off, measure the amount and recalculate the spacing distance. Once you have the spacing right, draw one of the corona circles on a poster board, cut it out, and use it as a template for drawing the corona.

17. Once you are done, pray and give thanks.

Labyrinths on the Land

As I mentioned earlier, the first outdoor labyrinth I ever created was for the Dominican Sisters retreat center in Saugerties, New York. Their meadow is large and I felt that a standard 40-foot Chartres type would look too small in the space, so I decided to double its size. Now, an 80-foot Chartres is a huge labyrinth. They wanted it completed by the weekend that a special retreat was planned, so I went up several weeks early to see the land, decide on the orientation, stake the center and the four quadrants, and be ready to complete it the day before the retreat.

When I arrived to complete the labyrinth, I was in for a surprise. It had never occurred to me how long it would take to do, nor that the grass would have grown. But grow it had. It was like waving grain, and so were all of my marker lines. Horrified, I accepted the kind sisters' invitation to have some lunch while the caretaker mowed the whole meadow, leaving only my center stake. That meant that I was left with less than six hours of daylight to complete the whole labyrinth. You have never seen anyone move so fast. Thank God I have such a good team of angels, for without their help I could never have done it. I spent the whole six hours bending over the lines, drawing until my fingers could barely hold onto the spray can. I ran out of paint and had to drive down to the local hardware store for refills. But by nightfall, I had a labyrinth minus the center petals and the corona, which I did manage to finish early the next morning. The trouble was that I was in such pain from all of the bending over that I could hardly move. I spent my fee on the massage therapist and the chiropractor when I got home.

That labyrinth is far from perfect, but it is perfectly beautiful to me. Maybe because of the gorgeous setting, maybe because of its wonderful energy, maybe because it was my first.

Much more so than with portable labyrinths, there are many things to consider before you put a labyrinth on the land. My general philosophy is, "The more labyrinths the better." But putting a permanent labyrinth is not an undertaking you enter into lightly. To build a permanent labyrinth, you should be able to answer these questions:

1. What is your intention in wanting a labyrinth? Do you have something specific in mind? What is it for?

2. How are you going to use the labyrinth? Is it for your own personal use? Will it be open to your family and/or your friends? Will it be open to the public? Will it be placed in a public place where it will be used a lot? Will it be available at all times?

3. Where are you going to put it? Do you have an available space? Do you know the dimensions you have to work with?

4. What materials are you going to use? Is there something readily available? How big is it going to be? What kind of labyrinth are you going to create? What direction is it going to face? What about maintaining it? Do you envision a permanent installation, or do you want to "try out" something temporary?

LESSONS FROM THE LABYRINTH

My colleague Marty Cain built a labyrinth in the backyard of a woman's house with a very particular use in mind. The client had cancer and had asked Marty for a labyrinth that would help with her healing. When the labyrinth was completed, some neighbors asked if they could walk it. "No," she said, "this labyrinth was intended only for my personal use. I'm sorry, you cannot walk it."

One day after she had returned from a trip, a man knocked on the woman's back door and announced he had walked her labyrinth while she had been away. Apparently he had a horrible experience, and told her she should get rid of it. "You had no right to walk my labyrinth without my permission," she replied. "I walk it every day and I leave my cancer in it."

This is a dramatic example of the power of our intentions and the importance of being clear about why you are creating your labyrinth and about what you want your labyrinth to do for you and any others who may walk it.

Direction and Orientation

After you have determined which labyrinth you are doing, the next issue is the orientation of the labyrinth. Which way will it face? The direction may have different meanings depending on your spiritual tradition. My preference is to have the entrance face east so that you are walking into the labyrinth from the east toward the west. In this cosmology, the East is the place of new beginnings, sunrises, and inspiration. I like to go toward the west, the direction of inner knowing and intuition.

The Chartres Cathedral is oriented in the exact opposite way. The west façade is the one with the three doors and the great rose window. You walk into the back of the cathedral at the west and then across the labyrinth and on up to the high altar, which is in the east—the place of the light. So you are walking from the place of darkness into the light.

There are times when placing the labyrinth on the land is fairly straightforward. Landscape elements or human structures may already be in place, and the labyrinth needs to be positioned in dialogue with whatever already exists on the land. Such was the case with the installation I made at the Dominican Sisters' retreat center. The center, which is situated on beautiful high land overlooking the Hudson River, is called Falling Waters. It's an appropriate name. A stream runs along one side of the meadow, where they wanted the labyrinth. On the far side, there is a grotto in which stands a statue of the Virgin Mary. As soon as I arrived, it was very clear to me that the labyrinth had to be oriented toward the grotto. People were not going to be happy walking into the center of the labyrinth and having their backs to the Virgin Mary. In this case, the question of orienting that labyrinth was solved long before I arrived.

Sometimes there aren't such constraints. All the choices, then, are open to you. This can actually make the process more challenging. In such a case, some people place the labyrinth to take advantage of the earth energies they perceive. I've come to believe that it's a good idea. One way to do this is through the ancient practice of dowsing. (A number of people involved in labyrinth work come from the dowsing tradition.) Although I don't consider myself to be a master dowser, I do use dowsing when placing and orienting a labyrinth on land. Dowsing is the art of determining the answers to specific questions by observing the movement of certain kinds of handheld instruments, such as rods or pendulums in responses to various energies. Like labyrinth walking, dowsing is an invitation to access our intuition, and to trust the process.

Some people pray or meditate over the question of where to locate a labyrinth. The most important thing is to know that what you are going to do is for the highest good. If at any point you get the sense that this labyrinth should not be built, then my advice is to stop and not continue it. You may want to meditate on the questions involved in constructing the labyrinth as well. For example, would it be for the highest good if this labyrinth were an eleven-circuit Chartres Cathedral labyrinth or a classical seven-circuit labyrinth?

Materials and Maintenance

After choosing the direction, determine the kind of *material* you are going to use. Temporary labyrinths can be mowed into grass or temporarily outlined with field-lining paint. The path can be marked with stakes and twine. (This is usually the first step in creating a permanent labyrinth in any case.) Selection of materials will have an impact on the width of the pathway as well as the width of the walls.

Labyrinth marked with stakes and twine.

The geometrical building blocks, or the materials from which you will construct the labyrinth, are key. Using forks or string on stakes means having a very small amount of space for the wall. Other materials may make a wider line for the walls, which makes a difference in terms of designing the labyrinth when you actually come to drawing it out. The final width of the walls, like the final width of the paths, are dimensions that must be determined in advance.

Using bricks laid out end to end makes for a narrow wall between the pathways, probably the narrowest material you can use in a permanently installed labyrinth. A brick is very thin, just over two inches wide. As a divider between the pathways, it will therefore take up less room than hedges or bushes would.

Rocks can also be used to outline the pathways. Of course, rocks vary

Brick labyrinth.

HELEN CURRY

greatly in size. The bigger the rock, the more room you'll need to account for between the pathways. This always expands the labyrinth outward.

What about the width of the pathway themselves? Part of your constraint is how much total space you have to work with, but there are other considerations as well. An experienced dowser wants to take into account the earth's energies in the most detailed way possible. He might actually dowse the location and width of each pathway. Using that method may result in pathways that don't end up being completely even and symmetrical. So the labyrinth and its asymmetries end up being far more organic in shape than something you might paint on a canvas or that you would create out of paving stones.

But perfectly geometric designs are probably not what you would want to come upon in the middle of a field. The organic asymmetries and slightly rougher designs are at home there. At the other end of the continuum, there are the beautiful and precise geometric configurations of the paved labyrinth. More fitting in an urban environment, these are often very expensive. They are very beautiful installations that can be done either in terrazzo or in paving stones. They are permanent and very carefully laid out. A good example is the one outside Grace Cathedral in San Francisco.

A labyrinth that I created for a private home on Long Island actually had a pathway that went around the back side of a tree. The labyrinth center was placed and the pathways spread out on one side in an ellipse to allow the tree to remain standing.

It is a lot of fun to use the existing topography in designing your labyrinth. It may be up and down a hill. It may have to go around trees or rock formations. I think those are all really lovely labyrinths. So you shouldn't be concerned with the geometry of it but rather with the energy of it. Even if it is not perfect, it is probably perfect for how you want to use it.

You also need to consider how the labyrinth is going to be used and main-

JAYNE BARON SHERMAN

A private labyrinth at a home on Long Island with a tree in the elliptical path.

tained. Some people are willing to spend a lot of time weeding the labyrinth, while others are not. Labyrinth paths outlined with rocks will require more upkeep and weed-trimming than one with bricks laid into the ground. At Saugerties, the creation of the labyrinth made with brick dug into the earth was fairly labor-intensive in the beginning. But once it was done, it could be mowed by the caretaker with a large mower that would go right across the top of it. He goes by with a weed whacker probably once a season because grass will overtake brick, but that's fairly minimal maintenance.

Cost is another consideration. I love to use "found" materials. In the case of the first labyrinth, the bricks were from an old icehouse on the property that was made of bricks that had fallen down into a pile of rubble. The bricks were there, and they were free. If you have the materials available, use what is at hand!

Once the labyrinth is complete, don't forget to give thanks for the opportunity to create this wonderful tool and open it with a blessing ceremony so that you can have a sacred space.

Labyrinth-building in the rain.

SISTER ADELE MEYERS

Nothing can replace the satisfaction of creating your own labyrinth, but putting a permanent labyrinth on the land can be a major commitment. Many members of the Labyrinth Society will consult with clients to help build labyrinths. If the logistics are too daunting for you to undertake it yourself, you can always find help.

Helen starting her stone labyrinth.

SISTER MARY REYNOLDS

LESSONS FROM THE LABYRINTH

For another outdoor Chartres labyrinth that I made for the Dominican Sisters at their Mother House in Sparkill, New York, it was decided that stones would fit in better than bricks with the stone architecture of the chapel nearby. Since any material we would use would need to be purchased, I met with the sisters in charge of the project and we made a trip to the local stone supplier to choose the stones. I found some beautiful, rather large ones that I thought would work very well. The sisters rejected them as being too big. Then I understood the most important thing was that we choose small enough stones so that all the sisters could lift them. This was another great lesson for me. I could so easily have just picked out those stones myself, and it would have been a disaster. They wanted to build their own. As it was, it poured rain the Saturday we built the labyrinth. We all got soaked and covered in mud, but we had a great time and built a terrific labyrinth—me and two dozen nuns, all by ourselves.

Epilogue: Beyond the Labyrinth

To take shape a journey must have fixed bearings, as a basket has ribs and a book its themes. The clearest way to understand . . . our journey . . . is to look at a single woven basket's basic design. . . . First, two splits or reeds are centered, like the cardinal points of a compass. Then, two more splits of equal size and length are added. These are the ribs of the basket. Weaving begins at the center . . . over . . . under . . . over . . . under until it is finished. From the simplest basket to the most complex . . . , this principle is the same: The ribs must be centered and held in balance. In a sense, they are the fixed bearings that guide the rhythm of the weaving.

—Marilou Awiakta:
Selu: Seeking the Corn-Mother's Wisdom

Like the ribs of the basket, the three-part journey of the labyrinth—the path in, the center, the path out—offers structure to the meditation. At its simplest, you prepare yourself on the journey in. You receive at the center. You accept and own what you have received on the journey out.

I acknowledge each of my readers for the courage to take the first step onto the labyrinth. And while it will meet you wherever you are on your journey, there is no telling where it may take you. Honor that. Try the walk again. And then again. In the end, why and how it works remains a great mystery.

The labyrinth is a metaphor for life: Once you get the patterns, the turns, the paths imprinted on your body, mind, feelings, and spirit, they will always be with you, like a spiritual tattoo.

You don't have to walk a labyrinth in some instances to see its profound workings and meanings of your daily life. I see a labyrinth metaphor in everything I do. For example, how is a tax form like the labyrinth? The Labyrinth Project of Connecticut, Inc., recently completed its five-year probation period with the Internal Revenue Service for its 501c3 nonprofit status. That means they will now look at our financial records for the last five years, and specifically at where our money has come from. I have visions of a form that will be like ten tax returns put together. When I called up my brother, who has been my financial advisor, he assured me that the form would take time to complete, but he also said, "Don't worry, there is a linear path through it."

I laughed. The truth of the matter is that I am not faced with a maze here. It's a labyrinth, and everything will be fine. All we have to do is put one foot in front of the other. We'll answer question 1, then question 2. I can cope with that.

That is the comfort of completing the tax form: That you *will* get to the end. No matter the twists and turns, there is a way out if you simply follow the path.

Start using the labyrinth, and soon you will begin to see everything in your life through its lens. You don't need special training. If I can do it, anybody can do it. I'm an ordinary woman. I don't have any advanced degree. My B.A. is in art history; I am not a therapist. Granted, I've been open to this kind of experience, and I came to the labyrinth after being in a meditation group for several years. But nothing prepared me for the power and inner growth that I have experienced through working with the labyrinth for seven years.

The labyrinth is one of the most compassionate and humane meditation tools available. It accesses all parts of what it means to be human. It is sacred space, yet it uses the body to pass through its pathways. It is a meditation tool that makes profound heart connections, yet it engages the rational mind as well. What integrative medicine is uncovering is that allopathic and alternative healing modalities used in conjunction with each other enhance the healing process. So too with the labyrinth. It works best when—and because—it works on all these levels simultaneously.

How Does the Labyrinth Work?

There is research in progress about how the labyrinth works and why. It certainly seems a worthy subject for continued investigation. There are many who are studying the healing effects of labyrinth walking on such diseases as multiple sclerosis, Parkinson's, and others. One theory relates to the labyrinth's twists and turns—the evenly symmetrical number of clockwise and counterclockwise 180-degree turns. Do these twists and turns have a balancing effect on the brain? Labyrinth Society member Richard Feather Anderson compares the twists and turns of the labyrinth to the alternating spiral patterns of water currents. We know that over time water purifies itself by the action of its currents when they are given free play to alternate their spiral patterns. Since humans are, after all, 70 percent water, might the turns be an important factor in purifying the body?

Perhaps the circular paths of the labyrinth form a kind of lens for focusing the power of intention and attention that is brought to the walk. The circle is the most basic form of all creation, and it is the basis for all of sacred geometry as well as for symbols from the collective unconscious the world over. There is no doubt that the inherent circular nature of the most popular labyrinth designs also plays an important role in how they work.

I think the most important reason the labyrinth works is because of our intention. On some level, most labyrinth walkers, either consciously or unconsciously, go into a labyrinth walk ready to receive something even if they are very skeptical. I believe the act of being ready to receive instantly opens up a channel for the universe to provide whatever is needed in the balancing, healing, or restoring that we might not even know we need.

There is a consciousness that grows out of the labyrinth, and that is created because the labyrinth is a divine space. It can be defined as divine, yet it is a space you can create and experience on the physical plane as well. The idea of sacred space can be set up in the blessing, even if it is just a simple blessing. Acknowledging that the labyrinth is a sacred space makes it feel different from a mall.

People can grasp this kind of meditation because it has a structure in physical space as well, like the ribs of a basket. You can look at it, walk on it. The pure physicality of locating the path in a place—even if that place is your piece of paper—allows for defining this as special or sacred space.

Beyond the physical presence of the path, understanding the meditation as a three-part journey helps people to experience major shifts. Consciously walking in preparation for receiving something allows something to happen, a shift, something to make a difference. That's not the same kind of consciousness that we have when we run down the street.

One of the extraordinary things for me personally was discovering that each walk is absolutely unique. I thought I would figure out someday that there are a limited number of labyrinth walks—say ten. Ten walks, ten experiences. But in fact there have never been two that are alike. Nor, after seven years of doing this work, have I come up with a way to predict what my labyrinth walk is going to be like on any given afternoon. I can't begin to predict. That's what's fun about it. There's that element of mystery and surprise and the unexpected *every single time.* I now get it, finally—that it is always going to be that way. Forty years from now I know it is going to be fresh and different every single time.

There is also a cumulative effect that you get when walking the labyrinth. As you start any kind of practice—yoga, Tai Chi, prayer, meditation, etc.— you begin as a beginner. You have a beginner's understanding of the experience. If you use the labyrinth for walking meditation, you build on the base of prior experiences.

In a practice such as Zen, it is always important to return to beginner's mind every time you do the sitting meditation. I liken this attitude to my admonition to labyrinth walkers to leave aside all expectation. It is easy to let an expectation based on how it was in a prior walk get in the way of experiencing *this* walk. Returning to a frame of mind without expectation is akin to returning to beginner's mind.

The labyrinth never changes. It is still paint on canvas, a path mowed into a meadow, or a groove in a wooden board. My colleague and fellow Labyrinth Society member Joe Miguez is fond of saying, "The labyrinth is a clear space." He means that it isn't loaded with "stuff" of its own. I like to say that the labyrinth meets us wherever we are on the path. That is why it is so universally effective.

Mysteries from the Labyrinth

An article about the labyrinth in the online magazine *Slate* recently made light of some women who walked the labyrinth at a spa and then, in a photograph, captured a shaft of rainbow light above the group as they stood together on the labyrinth for the shot. "It must have been a sun flare, something wrong with your camera," said all those rational minds seeking reasonable answers. When it comes to labyrinths, I don't count out other realms.

The very first walk we did on the Chartres-style labyrinth at the Norwalk Armory was captured on video as documentation of that project. We'd

The best response to mystery is vigilance and attentive waiting.
—Kathleen Norris

finished painting a day early and invited all the volunteers to come and walk on the labyrinth. We captured someone on that video who none of us had ever seen before nor have we since. Nobody saw her arrive, nobody saw her leave. She didn't sign in. No one who was there knew who she was. But there she is on that video, walking the labyrinth. And she's never shown up for a walk again. I thought that someday I would run into her somewhere. But, no, never. Although she looks very real and solid in the film, I've decided that she's an angel.

Another time, I needed to get a black-and-white shot of the seven-circuit labyrinth to advertise a workshop. It was the afternoon before a scheduled evening walk—dreary, gray, and rainy, as it often is in November. Three high school boys came to help move the chairs in the church and lay out the labyrinths for our All Saints' Day walk. I asked if they would mind walking the labyrinth so I could get shots of people walking. They agreed and I started shooting from all angles around the church. Despite the warning in the camera's viewfinder that I didn't have enough light, I continued to shoot without the flash until the whole roll was complete. When I got the developed pictures back, we had some fine shots of the labyrinth. But on several there seemed to be something else going on—an overlay of bubbles or Ping-Pong balls. In a couple of shots it was just a hint, but in several, it was almost as though you could see a three-dimensional grid of bubbles emanating up from the labyrinth. And in one shot, there seemed to be half a face next to the image of the bubbles. I have been told on good authority that the bubbles represent the energy grid that is created by the labyrinth. I have since learned that I am not the only person to capture otherworldly beings or energies in labyrinth photos. My colleagues Judith Joyce and John Wayne Blasingame have photos like these as well.

Our minds have been trained to be rational, linear, and scientific—probably too much so! We have devalued the mysterious. The resurgence of labyrinth walking, I think, is one way that people today are reclaiming the

*Mysterious bubble
images.*

mysterious. It's reopening the way for the numinous to return to our lives. Even scientists are becoming more open to alternative ways of knowing. There is a story told about the famous ballerina Pavlova, who, when asked to explain the meaning of a dance she had just performed, replied, "If I could have explained it to you I would not have needed to dance it." This is true for walking the labyrinth. And, to some degree, it is true of life itself. Words fall short. We limit things when we try to explain them through words. Sometimes, you simply need to experience. To know what the experience of walking the labyrinth is like, you need to walk the labyrinth.

Questions for the Journey

1. In what ways do you want to honor the experience of your labyrinth walks?

2. Have you observed any cumulative effects in your life after walking the labyrinth multiple times?

3. In what ways has the labyrinth worked for you?

4. Have you encountered any mysteries? Are you open to them?

LABYRINTH DIRECTORY

ALABAMA

The Labyrinth Project of Alabama
Contact: Annette Reynolds
204 Oak Road
Birmingham, AL 35216-1410
205-979-1744
AnetRey@aol.com
　　Semipublic; call for availability;
canvas, indoor, portable

Episcopal Church of the Redeemer
Contact: Camille Hegg
1100 South Cody Road
Mobile, AL 36695
334-639-1948
　　Public; always open; grass, outdoor, permanent

Ashworth Gate Labyrinth
Built by: Annette Reynolds
Contact: Terri Hill Geer
McCalla, AL 35111
205-477-7801
　　Semipublic; available by ap-
pointment or events; outdoor

44 ft., Santa Rosa labyrinth, pine
bark paths with brick

ARIZONA

Lanser Labyrinth
Built by: Taffy Lanser
Contact: Taffy Lanser
P.O. Box 4665
Cave Creek, AZ 85327
480-488-0085
tl@inficad.com
　　Semipublic; by appointment or
open house; 42 ft., seven-path,
classical style, quartz rock
　　Completed: 1995

"L'Overture"
Built by: Taffy Lanser
Contact (owner): Evaline Horrell
Beaver Creek, AZ 86335
520-567-9125
imagineart@sedona.net
　　Public; by appointment; classi-
cal river rock

**Labyrinth at the "Casa" (Franciscan
　　Renewal Center)**
Built by: Taffy Lanser
5802 E. Lincoln Dr.
Scottsdale, AZ 85253
480-948-7460
　　Public; always open; 42 ft.,
seven-path, classical, river rock
　　Completed: April 1998

Open Sky Labyrinth
Built by: Taffy Lanser and the Gar-
dens for Humanity
Contact: The Lodge at Sedona
125 Kallof Place
Sedona, AZ 86336
520-204-1942
　　Public; call for availability; 62
ft., seven-path, classical, river rock
　　Completed: May 1998

Unity Church Labyrinth
Built by: Taffy Lanser
Contact: Church office
1500 E. Greenway Parkway
Phoenix, AZ 85022
602-978-3200

Public; call for availability;
62 ft., seven-path, classical, river
rock
Planned for completion: October 2000

ARKANSAS

**Walking with the Saints
Labyrinth**
Built by: Robert Ferré
Contact: Mary L. Miller
St. Paul's Episcopal Church
224 N. East St.
Fayetteville, AR 72701
501-442-7373 or 501-443-4479
mlmiller@arkansasusa.com
Semipublic; call for availability; canvas
Completed: November 1999

CALIFORNIA

The Living Labyrinth
Designed by: Alex Champion,
built by Alex, friends, and
volunteers
Contact: Susan Brennan
6728 Langley Canyon Rd.
Prunedale, CA 93907
831-663-2052
gappyfarm@compuserve.com
Semipublic; always open;
75 ft., five-ring Chartres-style,
earthwork
Completed: March 1998

A Left-Hand Cretan Labyrinth
Built by: Alex Champion,
Petaluma Area Chamber of Commerce Leadership Class of 1999
Contact: Carolyn M. Carnell
Oak Hill Park
Howard Street
Petaluma, CA 94952
cmc@svn.net
Public; always open; rock
with sand
Completed: June 1999

Three-Ring Chartres
Project sponsored by the City of
Oakland
Built by: Alex Champion
Contact: Alex Champion
Lake Merritt
Oakland, CA 94610
707-895-3375
earthsymbols@earthlink.net
Public; always open; earthwork with rock path
Completed: March 1992

**Alex Champion's Private
Labyrinths**
Built by: Alex Champion
Contact: Alex Champion
19020 Gschwend Road
Philo, CA 95466
707-895-3375
earthsymbols@earthlink.net
Private; by appointment only;
seven variations including double
spiral two-ring Cretan, vesica
triangle
Completed: 1987 to 1999

Pinwheel Maze in Chinese Playground
Built by: Alex Champion, Joan
Champion, and North Bay Courts
of Napa
Contact: Alex Champion
Sacramento Street, between
Grant and Stockton
San Francisco, CA
707-895-3375
earthsymbols@earthlink.net
Public; available during the
day; outdoor, permanent
Completed: April 1998

Right-Hand Cretan Labyrinth
Built by: Helena Mazzariello,
Alex Champion, Nac Ballard, and
members of the public
Contact: Alex Champion
Sibley Volcanic Regional
Preserve
Oakland, CA
707-895-3375
earthsymbols@earthlink.net
Public; available during the
day; stone, outdoor, permanent
Completed: 1992

Mandala Labyrinth Center
Contact: Sue Anne Foster
5204 Winding Way
Carmichael, CA 95608
916-486-3745
Mandala33@aol.com
Semipublic; open for scheduled events; garden, outdoor
Also three portable
labyrinths: 15-ft. canvas, 26-ft.

ivy path on canvas, 36 ft. Healing
Earth Tree
   Completed: September 1997

Christ the King Lutheran Church
Built by: Alain Degand
Contact: Pastor Dale Krumland or
Georgiana Lofty, labyrinth facilitator
2706 West 182nd Street
Torrance, CA 90504
310-323-6821 or Georgiana Lofty:
562-439-6595
g@sacredwalk.com
   Public; Monday through Friday
9 A.M. to 4 P.M. and by appointment; inlaid stone, indoor, permanent
   Completed: April 1998

Cretan Seven-Circuit Labyrinth
Built by: Annemarie Rawlinson
Contact: Annemarie Rawlinson
29214 Trotwood Ave.
Rancho Palos Verdes, CA 90275
310-832-9767
edkubis@earthlink.net
   Public; open for scheduled
events; canvas, indoor, portable
   Completed: 1998

Vesica Triangle at the Cancer Prevention and Treatment Center of the Central Coast of California
Built by: Alex Champion
Contact: Jennifer J. Choate, M.D.
3035 Main Street
Soquel, CA 95073
831-462-8750

JJChoate@aol.com
   Semipublic; by appointment;
earthwork, outdoor
   Completed: September 1998

Church of St. Gregory of Nyssa
Contact: Donald Schell
500 DeHaro Street
San Francisco, CA 94107-2316
415-255-8100
donald.schell@ecunet.com
   Semipublic; call for availability;
wood, indoor
   Completed: 1996

Veriditas
Built by: Lauren Artress
Contact: Tom Keelan
Grace Cathedral
1100 California Street
San Francisco, CA 94108
415-749-6358
   Public; two labyrinths available;
wool tapestry, indoor, permanent,
call for availability; terrazzo, outdoor, permanent, always open

California Pacific Medical Center
Built by: Victoria Stone
Contact: Victoria Stone
2333 Buchanan Street at Clay
San Francisco, CA 94115
415-826-0904
victoria@stonecircledesign.com
   Public; always open; All Deck
Painted Coating System, outdoor,
permanent (the first to be placed in
a hospital setting)
   Completed: June 1997

Labyrinth of Life: The West County Community Services Sebastopol Teen Center's Santa Rosa Labyrinth
Built by: Lea Goode, Jeffrey Edelheit, De'Anna L'am, and the Sebastopol teens and community
Contact: Program Director
425 Morris Avenue
Sebastopol, CA 95472
707-575-7570
   Public; always available; brick
and sod, outdoor, permanent
   Completed: June 1999

Fairfax Community Church
Contact: Sara Vurek
2398 Sr. Francis Drake Blvd.
Fairfax, CA 94930
415-454-6085
   Call for event information

St. Cross by the Sea Episcopal Church
Contact: Tom Murdock
1818 Monterey Ave.
Hermosa Beach, CA 90254
310-376-8989
tpm884@aol.com.
   Portable

Trinity Episcopal Church
Contact: Allison Jaqua
1500 State St.
Santa Barbara, CA 93101
805-963-7976

St. Paul's Cathedral
Contact: James Langston
2728 Sixth Ave.
San Diego, CA 92103
619-298-7261

Christ Unity Church
Contact: Pat Casey
9429 Folsom Blvd.
Sacramento, CA 95826
916-990-0236
pkcd1111@aol.com
    Public; open first Sunday of
each month from 5 P.M. to 7 P.M.;
Chartres-style, canvas
    Completed: April 1997

**Carmel Valley Community
    Chapel**
Contact: Elizabeth Carlson
Corner of Paso Hondo and Village Drive
Carmel Valley, CA 93924
831-659-2278, or Elizabeth Carlson: 831-659-4054
    Public; always open; seven-
circuit, 33-ft.-diameter classical,
river rock and pea gravel, outdoor, permanent

Friendly Hills Labyrinth
Built by: James Beal and
Roberta Shoemaker-Beal
Friendly Hills Ranch
28195 Fairview Ave.
Hemet, CA 92544
909-927-1768, Fax: 909-927-
1548

Semipublic; call for arrangements; earth and stones, outdoor,
permanent
    Completed: July 1997

COLORADO

Unity Labyrinth Project
Contact: Marlene Moody
3021 S. University Blvd.
Denver, CO 80210
303-758-5664 or 303-758-5665
    Indoor, canvas

CONNECTICUT

**The Labyrinth Project of Con-
necticut, Inc.**
Contact: Helen Curry
PO Box 813
New Canaan, CT 06840
203-966-5459
director@CTlabyrinth.org
    Public; open for scheduled
events; three canvas, indoor,
portable

Ann Ameling's Labyrinth
Built by: Robert Ferré
Contact: Ann Ameling
869 Orange Street
New Haven, CT 06511
203-624-8894

ann.ameling@yale.edu
    Call for availability; can be
rented; canvas Chartres

Mercy Center
Built by: Eugenie Guterch, RSM
Contact: Eugenie Guterch, RSM
167 Neck Road,
Madison, CT 06443
203-245-0401
    Semipublic; call for appoint-
ment; brick and boxwood walls,
stony creek granite path
    Completed: 1998

Journey of the Heart
Built by: Robert Ferré
Contact: Cathie LeVasseur
239 Sasco Hill Road
Fairfield, CT 06430
203-255-0585
    Available upon request; 35-ft.
portable Chartres on canvas

Christ Church Cathedral
Contact: Dick Mansfield
45 Church Street
Hartford, CT 06103
860-527-7231
    Public; always open; grass,
outdoor, permanent

Wisdom House
Contact: Rosemarie Greco, DW
229 E. Litchfield Road
Litchfield, CT 06759-3002
860-567-3163

Private; call for availability; brick-and-stone seven-circuit

DELAWARE

First and Central Presbyterian Church
Contact: Rev. Vin Harwell
1101 Market Street
Wilmington, DE 19801
302-654-5371
Private; open for scheduled events; canvas, indoor, portable

St. Peter's Episcopal Church
Contact: Mary Van House
Second and Market Street
Lewes, DE 19958
302-684-1652
Private; open for scheduled events; canvas, indoor, portable

Unitarian Universalist Fellowship of Newark
Contact: Rev. Greg Chute
420 Willa Road
Newark, DE 19711
302-368-2984

FLORIDA

Unity of Naples
Built by: Chuck Hunner

2000 Unity Way
Naples, Florida 34112
941-775-3009
info@goldenspirit.com
Public; call for availability; 28 ft., seven-circuit, reef rock, outdoor, permanent
Completed: February 2000

The Cenacle Retreat Center
Built by: Gundela Freidman, Pat Reames, and others
Contact: Sr. Peggy Lane or Sr. Elizabeth
1400 S. Dixie Highway
Lantana, FL 33462
561-582-2534
CenacleFL@aol.com.
Public; always open; concrete stones, outdoor, permanent
Completed: June 1999

The Church of the Good Shepherd
Built by: Gilson Campos, Jr.
Contact: Rev. Wendy Williams
400 Seabrook Rd.
Tequesta, FL 33469
561-746-4674
www.web-edge.com/labyrinth
Public; call for availability; hand-cast concrete pieces, outdoor, permanent

Woodlawn Memorium, Memorial Park and Funeral Home
Contact: Jeanne Miller-Clark
555 West State Road 434
Longwood, FL 32750

407-767-1200, ext. 5583
Public; daily from 7 A.M. to sunset; painted concrete, outdoor, permanent

Private Labyrinth
Contact: Robert G. Neel
P.O. Box 585627
Orlando, FL 32858-5627
407-649-6480
Private; open for scheduled events; canvas, indoor, portable

Private Labyrinth
Contact: Aimee Dominique
4200 Community Drive #709
Palm Beach, FL 33409
561-712-0641
Private; open for scheduled events; canvas, indoor, portable

Passe-a-Grille Beach Community Church
Contact: Emily Bell
107 16th Ave.
St. Pete Beach, FL 33706
727-360-5508
Public; always open; outdoor, permanent

Future Health Concepts
Contact: Patricia Brown
4994 Picciola Road
Fruitland Park, FL 34749
352-787-0313
Private; call for availability; canvas, indoor, portable

GEORGIA

Alexzanna Farms Labyrinth
Built by: Annette Reynolds
Contact: Suzanna Alexander
Wildwood, GA 30757
706-820-9042
  Semipublic; always available
by appointment; outdoor seven-
circuit classical, flagstone and
grass paths
  Completed: 1997

Cathy and Monte Ray
Built by: Marty Cain
P.O. Box 2705
Blairsville, GA 30514
704-389-3751 or 706-745-3008
  Public; seven-circuit path
marked with stones, outdoor,
permanent
  Completed: June 1996

Sonia Gage
Built by: Marty Cain
P.O. Box 240
Winterville, GA 03683
706-724-2210
  Public; by appointment;
seven-circuit path marked with
stones, outdoor, permanent
  Completed: November 1996

Juli Wilson
Built by: Marty Cain
1261 Preacher Campbell Rd.
Clarksville, GA 30523

706-754-8592
earthstick@aol.com
  Public; call for availability;
seven-circuit, Cretan-style, grass,
outdoor, permanent
  Completed: April 1998

Mary Zorn Bates
Built by: Marty Cain
1291 Da Andrea Dr.
Watkinsville, GA 30677
706-353-0709
  Public; open for scheduled
events; seven-circuit classical
marked with flags, tape, and
stones, outdoor
  Completed: April 1998

S. Thompson
Built by: Marty Cain
Watkinsville, GA 03677
706-769-5498
  Public; seven-circuit classical
path, permanent
  Completed: 1998

Lillian Hall
Built by: Marty Cain
43 Leigh's Crossing
Cleveland, GA 30528
706-219-4791
  Public; seven-circuit classical
path marked with fieldstones,
permanent
  Completed: February 1998

Holy Trinity Parish
Contact: Susan Latimer
515 E. Ponce de Leon Ave.
Decatur, GA 30030
404-377-2622
  Public; always open; outdoor,
permanent

Private Labyrinth
Contact: Carl Cofer
1121 Walden Rd.
Chickamauga, GA 30707
706-539-1457
  Public; always open; canvas,
indoor, portable

Church of the Good Shepherd
Contact: Daniel Brown
2230 Walton Way
Augusta, GA 30904
706-728-3386
  Public; always open; canvas,
indoor, portable

**Park Memorial United Methodist
  Church**
Contact: Dan Johnston
5290 Arkwright Road
Macon, GA 31210
912-633-1351
  Public; always open; outdoor,
permanent

Public Labyrinth
Contact: Stan White
3424 N. Valdosta Rd.
Valdosta, GA 31602
912-247-6859

Public; open for scheduled events; canvas, indoor, portable

Episcopal Diocese of Georgia
Contact: Nancy Mills
907 N. Dawson Street
Thomasville, GA 31792
912-226-2735
Public; call for availability; canvas, indoor, portable

The Cathedral of St. Phillip: Buckhead
2744 Peachtree Road, NW
Atlanta, GA 30305
404-365-1000
www.accessatlanta.com/community/groups/stphillip/Labyrinth_Part_of_Wo.html
Public; available for use by outside groups at their location every Friday evening from 3 P.M. to 8 P.M.; canvas, 35-ft. diameter, eleven-circuit, Chartres-style, indoor

Holy Innocents' Episcopal Church
805 Mount Vernon Hwy.
Atlanta, GA 30327
404-255-4023
www.holyinnocents.org
Public; open on the first Monday of each month from 4 P.M. to 8 P.M.; canvas, 35-ft. diameter, eleven-circuit, Chartres-style, indoor

Innovox: A Connectivity Lounge
Contact: Jeff Ford
699 Ponce de Leon Ave, Suite 1
Atlanta, GA 30308
404-872-4482
innovox@aol.com
http://www.innovoxlounge.com
Public; open every Sunday from 2:30 P.M. to 4:00 P.M.; painted concrete, 19-ft. diameter, seven-circuit, Cretan-style, indoor

Prince of Peace Lutheran Church
Contact: Pastor Keith
257 Highway 314
Fayetteville, GA 30214
770-461-3403
poplc@unidial.com
Public; open year-round; 48-ft. diameter, seven-circuit, Cretan-style, brick and earth, outdoor, permanent

Park Memorial United Methodist Church
5290 Arkwright Road
Macon, GA 31210
912-471-1008
Public; open year-round; 45-ft. diameter, seven-circuit, Cretan-style, natural earth and stone, outdoor

St. Francis Episcopal Church
532 Forest Hill Road
Macon, GA 31210
912-477-4616

Public; open year-round; 40-ft. diameter, seven-circuit, Cretan-style, natural earth and stone, outdoor

St. Thomas Episcopal Church
Contact: Nancy Byars
216 Remington Ave.
Thomasville, GA 31792
912-226-6614
http://home.rose.net/~stthomas
Public; open on the second Saturday of each month from 10 A.M. to 9 P.M.; available for use by outside groups at their location, canvas, 32-ft. diameter, eleven-circuit, Chartres-style, indoor

The Atlanta Labyrinth
Built by: Bob Peach
Duluth, GA
bsp@avana.net
Available for use by church groups and for other spiritual services; e-mail for arrangements; canvas (20 × 22 ft.), seven-circuit, Chartres-style, indoor
Completed: December 1998

Lookout Mountain, Hawks Above Spiritual Retreat Center
Contact: Bo Hawk
606 Valley View Ranch Rd.
Cloudland, GA 30731
706-862-2231
BoHawk8533@aol.com
www.hawksabove.com

Private; by appointment; natural earth and stone, seven-circuit, Cretan-style, outdoor

HAWAII

St. John's Church
RR2, Box 212
Kula, HI 96790
808-878-1485 or 808-878-6974
janetm@aloha.net
Outdoor labyrinth

Healing Heart Foundation
Built by: Neal Pinckney
Contact: Neal Pinckney
84-683 Upena Street
Makaha, HI 96792
808-696-2428
heart@aloha.net
Semiprivate; often available; painted concrete, outdoor, permanent
Completed: November 1998

Latifa Amdur
Built by: Marty Cain
P.O. Box 1232
Hanalei, Kauai, HI 96714
808-828-1155
lam@aloha.net
Public; call for availability; seven-circuit path marked with sticks and string, permanent
Completed: February 1998

ILLINOIS

St. Charles Episcopal Church Labyrinth
Built by: Tecza Environmental Group of Elgin, IL
Contact: Cathy Koch, Beth Parks, Mary Elfring
994 North Fifth Ave.
St. Charles, IL 60174
630-584-2596
Public; always open; granite cobblestones, crushed limestone
Completed: October 1997

St. James Episcopal Cathedral
Built by: Robert Ferré
65 E. Huron St.
Chicago, IL 60611
312-787-7360
Public; call for availability; permanent outdoor and a portable canvas; labyrinth available for loan

Earth-Wisdom Labyrinth
Built by: Neal Harris and Unitarian Universalist church members
Contact: Judi Mason at 312-527-5488 or Dan Brosier
Unitarian Universalist Church
Elgin, IL 60120
847-888-0668
info@relax4life.com
Public; available sunrise through sunset daily and later evenings by appointment; 94 ft.,

fieldstone laid atop landscape cloth, Chartres-style, outdoor
Completed: June 1997

Private Labyrinth
Contact: Mary Klein
20112 Hebron Rd.
Harvard, IL 60033
262-248-1916 or 815-943-4765
Public; open every day during daylight hours; prairie-style

Naperville Millennium Labyrinth
Built by: Marty Kermeen
Contact: Marty or Debi Kermeen
Naperville Riverwalk, corner of Eagle St. and Jefferson
Naperville, IL 60545
630-552-3408
artpaver@aol.com
Public; always open; concrete paving stones
Completed: September 1998

INDIANA

Greencastle Labyrinth Meditation Path
Contact: Gwen Bottoms
Greencastle, IN 46135
765-653-3921
Private; open 8 A.M. to 6 P.M.; painted concrete, outdoor, permanent

The Hermitage
Contact: Bill Coleman
3650 East 46th Street
Indianapolis, IN 46205
317-545-0742
Private; call for availability;
canvas, indoor, portable

The Church of Nativity
7300 Lantern Road
Indianapolis, IN 46256
317-849-3656
Private; call for availability;
canvas, indoor, portable

**St. Luke's University Medical
Center**
100 W. 86th St.
Indianapolis, IN 46260
317-846-3404
Public; open for scheduled
events; canvas, indoor, portable

**Waycross Episcopal Camp and
Conference Center**
Contact: Gene Niednagel
7363 Bear Creek Road
Morgantown, IN 46460
812-597-4241
Public, always open; canvas, in-
door, portable

**Epworth Forest Conference and
Retreat Center**
P.O. Box 16
North Webster, IN 46555
800-834-9873

Public, call for availability;
grass, outdoor, permanent

Oakwood Spiritual Life Center
Contact: Judy Homer
702 E. Lake View Road
Syracuse, IN 46567
219-457-5781, ext. 425
Public; call for availability; canvas, indoor, portable

Epworth United Methodist Church
Contact: Lawrence VanVactor-Lee
5311 Hessen Cassel
Fort Wayne, IN 46806
219-447-4211
Public; always open; grass,
outdoor, permanent

Sophia's Portico
Contact: Margaret Hoffelder
2000 N. Wells, Bldg. #1
Fort Wayne, IN 46808
219-423-4770
Public; always open; grass, outdoor, permanent

Corydon Presbyterian Church
Contact: David Cliburn
568 Highway 62 West
Corydon, IN 47112
812-738-3929
Public; call for availability; seed
kit, indoor, portable

Geneva Center
Contact: Terri Michaelis
Rochester, IN 46975
219-223-6915
Public; call for availability;
outdoor, permanent

**Cathedral Labyrinth and Sacred
Garden**
Contact: Karen Chadwick
310 North Street
New Harmony, IN 47631
812-682-3050
Public; always open; outdoor,
permanent

IOWA

United Christian Campus Ministry
Contact: Rev. Beverly A. Thomp-
son-Travis
200 Lynn Ave.
Ames, IA 50014
515-292-3823
Private; call for availability;
grass, outdoor, permanent

Mellineum
Contact: Kathy Hankel
217 East Lincoln Way
Jefferson, IA 50129
515-386-2280
Private; call for availability;
canvas, indoor, portable

Private Labyrinth
Contact: Saundra Strong
9295 N.W. 41st Court
Des Moines, IA 50226
515-964-5334
Public; open for scheduled events; canvas, indoor, portable

Private Labyrinth
Contact: Dorothy Whiston
317 Mahaska Drive
Iowa City, IA 52246
319-339-7305
Private; call for availability; canvas, indoor, portable

KANSAS

College Hill United Methodist Church
Contact: Rev. Gary Collins
2930 East First Street
Wichita, KS 37214-4784
316-683-4649
Private; call for availability; canvas, indoor, portable

KENTUCKY

Sacred Oak Grove
Built by: Joyce Fitzgerald, Gary Beilfeld, Clarice O'Bryan
Contact: Clarice O'Bryan
2504 Highway 1554

Owensboro, KY 42301
270-771-4737
ClarCoach@aol.com
Semipublic; call for availability; sandstone
Completed: 1998

Harrods Creek Farm
Contact: Eleanor and Rowland Miller
1000 N. Highway 1694
Goshen, KY 40026
502-584-5100
Private; call for availability; outdoor, permanent

The Ark Retreat
Contact: Theresa Scherf
147 Barrett Lane
Berea, KY 40403
606-985-7419
Private; call for availability; canvas, outdoor, portable

Danville Labyrinth Project
Built by: Local volunteers
Contact: Shelley Richardson
Main Street
Danville, KY 40422
606-332-4201
labyrinth@elmwoodinn.com
Public; available on the first Sunday through Tuesday each month; one canvas, one sheerweave, both portable
Completed: 1999

Moye Spiritual Life Center
Contact: Mary Jo Hummeldorf
Melbourne, KY 41059
606-441-0700, ext. 327
Private; call for availability; canvas, indoor, portable

LOUISIANA

Spiritual Journeys
Contact: Aimée Dominique
655 Marie Antoinette
Lafayette, LA 70506
337-984-3808
Sacredsteps4@aol.com.
Private; call for availability; indoor, portable
Completed: 1996

MAINE

Judy and Rodney Reading
Built by: Marty Cain
Battleridge Road
Box 390
Clinton, ME 04927
207-462-2964
Public; seven-path classical marked with flags and tape, permanent
Completed: 1994

Susan Monday-Wyman
111 Norton Road
Kittery, ME 03904
207-439-0055

Public; always open; outdoor, permanent

Bates College Chaplain's Office
Contact: Kerry Maloney
163 Wood St.
Lewiston, ME 04240
207-786-8272
Public; open for scheduled events; canvas, indoor, portable

H'ArtWorks
Contact: Jo-an Jacobus
728 Millay Road
Bowdoin, ME 04287
207-666-3995
Private; call for availability; canvas, indoor, portable

Private Labyrinth
Contact: Terry Rankine
P.O. Box 281
South Thomaston, ME 04858
207-596-0668
Private; call for availability; grass, outdoor, permanent

MARYLAND

Unity Christ Church
Contact: Allen Quay
111 Central Avenue
Gaithersburg, MD 20877
301-840-0207
Public; call for availability; canvas, indoor, portable

Hesychia Spiritual Center at Gloria Dei
Contact: Carol Leach
461 College Parkway
Arnold, MD 21012
410-544-6832
Public; call for availability; canvas, indoor, portable

Mount Vernon Place United Methodist Church
Contact: Pamela Wicklein
10 E. Mt. Vernon Place
Baltimore, MD 21202
410-561-7555
Public; call for availability; indoor, portable

Govans Presbyterian Church
Contact: Jack Sharp
5828 York Road
Baltimore, MD 21212
410-435-9188
Private; always open; grass, outdoor, permanent

Forestheart Studio
Contact: Mary Klotz
200 S. Main Street, Box 112
Woodsboro, MD 21798
301-845-4447
Private; always open; painted concrete, outdoor, permanent

MASSACHUSETTS

Kenton Tharp and Linda Kaiser
Built by: Marty Cain
371 Montague Rd.
Amherst, MA 01002
413-549-6215
Public; seven-path, grass, outdoor, permanent

Somerville Arts Council
Contact: Jeff Chelgren, Somerville Planning Dept.
Built by: Marty Cain
Vinal Street
Somerville, MA
Mailing address: 93 Highland Ave.
Somerville, MA 02143
Public; inlaid brick in turf, seven-path classical, outdoor, permanent
Completed: March 1994

Church of St. Andrew
Built by: Marty Cain
Contact: Rev. Howard W. Gamble and Sarah Lincoln Harrison
135 Lafayette Street
Marblehead, MA 01945
617-631-4951
Public; always open; seven-path labyrinth marked with sand and beach stones, outdoor, permanent
Completed: 1994

Elizabeth Stoe
Built by: Marty Cain

309 Mountain Valley Rd.
Great Barrington, MA 02130
413-528-3979
   Public; seven-path marked with stone, permanent
   Completed: September 1995

Elizabeth Wheeler and Arunima Orr
Built by: Marty Cain
55 Page Rd.
Lincoln, MA 01773
617-259-0223
   Public; call for availability; seven-path made by digging out the paths and creating raised mounds between, permanent
   Completed: October 1996

Gwen Broz
Built by: Marty Cain
P.O. Box 4
West Brookfield, MA 01585
508-867-9810
   Public; by appointment; seven-path marked with stones, permanent
   Completed: 1996

St. Paul's Cathedral
Contact: Jep Streit, pastor
Built by: Marty Cain
138 Tremont St.
Boston, MA 02111
617-482-5800, ext. 203
   Public; seven-path classical, stained into wood on floor directly below nave of church, permanent
   Completed: 1996

Mary-ann Martin
Built by: Marty Cain
1162 Nantasket Ave.
Hull, MA 02045
781-925-3101
   Public; five-path classical marked with ocean rocks, permanent
   Completed: 1997

Rowe Camp and Conference Center
Contact: Prue Berry
Built by: Marty Cain
King's Highway Road
Rowe, MA 01367
   Public; seven-path labyrinth marked with stones, permanent
   Completed: November 1998

Irene Young
Built by: Marty Cain
(located in Pocasset, MA)
P.O. Box 1559
North Falmouth, MA 02556
508-563-2159
   Public; five-path classical marked with beach stones, permanent
   Completed: May 1998

ARA Wellness Center
Contact: Terry Andrews and Maryann Keefe
Built by: Marty Cain
349 Baldwinville Rd.
Templeton, MA 01468
978-939-4437

Public; call for availability; seven-path classical marked with rocks, permanent
   Completed: August 1999

Annie's Garden and Gift Store
Contact: Annie Cheatham
515 Sunderland Road
Amherst, MA 01002
413-549-6359
   Public; always open; outdoor, permanent

Granville Citizen's Park
Corner of Routes 57 and 189
Granville, MA 01034
   Public; always open; outdoor, permanent

Leominster Labyrinth
Contact: Susan McNeill
64 West Street
Leominster, MA 01453
978-840-3093
   Public; always open; painted concrete, outdoor, permanent

Congregational Church of West Medford
Contact: Rev. Kathryn Titus
400 High Street
Medford, MA 02155
781-391-1527
   Public; call for availability; indoor, permanent

Sacred Space Workshops
Contact: Patti Keeler
179 Church Street
East Harwich, MA 02645
508-432-0797
    Private; call for availability;
canvas, indoor, portable

Boston College
Contact: Prof. Rebecca Valette
College Rd. and Commonwealth
Ave.
Newton (Chestnut Hill), MA 10467
617-552-3825
    Public; always open; outdoor,
grass, outdoor, permanent

MICHIGAN

Morning Star Chartres Labyrinth
Built by: Elise Schlaikjer, Julie
Keefer, and Mark Maier
Contact: Elise Schlaikjer
20564 Morning Star Trail
LeRoy, MI 49655
231-768-4869 or 231-768-4368
roselise@netonecom.net
    Semipublic; call for availability;
stone, outdoor
    Completed: 1998

**Orchard Ridge Campus/Oakland
    Community College**
Contact: Robert Pripenburg
27055 Orchard Lake Rd.
Farmington Hills, MI 48018
248-471-7711

    Private; call for availability;
canvas, indoor, portable

The First Congregational Church
Contact: Rev. Robert A. Martin
P.O. Box 5, 102 Church Street
Romeo, MI 48065
810-752-3661
    Public; call for availability; can-
vas, indoor, portable

Henry Ford Community College
Contact: Maggie Anderson
5101 Evergreen
Dearborn, MI 48128
734-997-0529
    Private; call for availability; in-
door, portable

Church of Our Savior
Contact: Dr. Louis S. Thompson
6655 Middlebelt Road
W. Bloomfield, MI 48322
248-626-7606
    Public; always open; two
labyrinths available: canvas, indoor,
portable—available for borrowing;
outdoor grass, permanent

**Episcopal Diocese of Western
    Michigan**
Contact: Elizabeth Tompkins
2600 Vincent Avenue
Portage, MI 49002
616-381-2731
    Public; always open; outdoor
grass, permanent

Private Labyrinth
Contact: Rev. Ruth Clausen
310 Quaintance
Petoskey, MI 49770
231-348-3422
    Private; call for availability;
canvas, indoor, portable

MINNESOTA

Trinity Labyrinth, Trinity Hospital
Built by: Lowell Russell Concrete
Inc.
Contact: Martha Erickson
3410 213th St.
Farmington, MN 55024-1197
651-463-7825
    Public; available, weather per-
mitting, spring, summer, fall; handicapped accessible; 42 ft.,
Chartres-style, cement, outdoor,
permanent
    Completed: October 1999

Martha Y. Erickson
Built by: Stuart Bartholomaus
Contact: Martha Y. Erickson
19833 Jersey Ave.
Lakeville, MN 55044
952-469-2317
Myerickson@aol.com
    Semipublic; by appointment
only, may be rented with or without presenter/owner; seven-circuit,
canvas, modified Chartres, indoor,
portable
    Completed: February 2000

Wisdom Ways Labyrinth
Built by: Stuart Bartholomaus
Contact: Wisdom Ways Resource
Center for Spirituality
1890 Randolph Ave.
St. Paul, MN 55105
651-690-8830
wisdomways@stkate.edu
  Public; available until winter;
seven-circuit, Chartres-style,
grass, outdoor, permanent
  Completed: May 1997

Private Labyrinth
Contact: Barbara Kellett
1479 Clarmar Avenue
Roseville, MN 55113
651-636-8419
  Private; call for availability;
canvas, indoor, portable

Christ Episcopal Church
Contact: Ian Lindridge
7305 Afton Road
Woodbury, MN 55125
651-735-8790
  Public; always open; grass,
outdoor, permanent

Private Labyrinth
Built by: Robert Ferré and Jill
K. H. Geoffrion and friends
Contact: Jill K. H. Geoffrion
18950 Northome Blvd.
Deephaven, MN 55391-2611
952-404-8268
jillkhg7@aol.com

Semipublic; call for availability; grass and brick, outdoor,
permanent
  Completed: May 1999

Clare's Well
13537-47th Street N.W.
Annandale, MN 55302
320-274-3512
  Private; call for availability;
grass, outdoor, permanent

MISSISSIPPI

Sissie Wile
Contact: Sissie Wile
5229 16th Ave.
Meridian, MS 39305
601-483-4054
  Private; call for availability;
canvas, indoor, portable

St. Andrews Mission, Inc.
Contact: Rev. Rich Hendricks
821-A LaBranch Street
McComb, MS 39648
601-684-4678
  Public; always open; grass,
outdoor, permanent

MISSOURI

The Prairie Labyrinth
Built by: Toby Evans and Mary K.
Barge
Contact: Toby Evans
1316 N. Holly Rd.
Sibley, MO 64088
816-650-5474
prairie@thinc.missouri.org
  Public; by appointment;
seven-circuit, 166 ft., grass, out-
door, permanent
  Completed: March 1995

MONTANA

The Portable School Labyrinths
Built by: Ginger Arnold, Tim
Rogers, and the Portable School
Main Street (Highway 3)
Lavina, Mt. 59046
406-636-2006
  Two available; seven-circuit
rainbow, chalk on cement; canvas
portable available for scheduled
events

Redsun Labyrinth
Built by: Patty and Helmut Meyer
Contact: Patty Meyer
1802 Pleasant View Dr.
Victor, MT 59875
406-642-6675
redsun@cybernet1.com

Private; available by appointment only; permanent labyrinth,
180 ft., fieldstones on grounds,
cloth
  Completed: November 1999

NEBRASKA

Right-Hand Cretan Labyrinth for the Prairie Peace Park
Built by: Alex Champion
Contact: Don Tilley
Prairie Peace Park (seven miles
west of Lincoln, NE)
402-795-2144
  Public; during the day, spring
through fall; 78 ft., earthwork covered with prairie grass, outdoor,
permanent
  Completed: October 1993

NEVADA

Haven Selah
Built by: Group effort led by Sue
Trumpfheller
Contact: Teresa Fuller
1680 N. Blagg Rd.
Pahrump, NV 89048
775-727-8633
havenselah@net-nerds.com
  Public; available most of the
time; stone
  Completed: October 1999

NEW HAMPSHIRE

Diocese of New Hampshire
Contact: Sean David Bennett
9 Petty Road
Wilton, NH 03086
603-654-5281
  Private; call for availability;
canvas, indoor, portable

InnerInk
Contact: Jim Vaillancourt
29 Pine Acres Road
Concord, NH 03301
603-225-5924
  Private; call for availability;
canvas, indoor, portable

Public Labyrinth
Contact: Penni Derby
447 Forest Lake Road
Winchester, NH 03470
603-239-6409
  Public; always open; outdoor,
permanent

Public Labyrinth
Michelle Kinsella
57 Long Hill Rd.
Raymond, NH 03077
603-895-9668
  Public; by appointment; seven-
circuit path marked with fieldstones, outdoor
  Completed: 1996

NEW JERSEY

Jersey City Alliance to Combat Drug and Alcohol Abuse
Contact: Bernadette Debbs
201 Comelisan Ave.
Jersey City, NJ 07304
201-432-4393
JAlliance@AOL.com
  Five-circuit 36-ft. Chartres-
style
  Built by: Robert Ferré
  26-ft. canvas rainbow Cretan
  Built by: Robert Ferré
  20-ft. nylon Cretan
  Built by: Pamela Ramadei
  17-ft. vinyl octagon-shaped
Chartres-style
  17-ft. Cretan world map
  There is also a small, three-cir-
cuit, canvas personal labyrinth.
  Public; call for availability—for
local use only; indoor, portable
  Completed: February 2000

The Labyrinth Walk at the Franklin Lakes Presbyterian Church
Built by: Robert Ferré
Contact: Pastor Jack Lohr or Joan
Ambrose
730 Franklin Lakes Road
Franklin Lakes, NJ 07417
201-891-0511 / 973-636-6360
pcfl@internexus.net
  Public; available usually the
fourth Saturday of the month between 10 A.M. and 4 P.M.; call first;
36-ft. Chartres on canvas
  Completed: March 2000

Crystal Labyrinth
Labyrinth Ways
45 Unneberg Avenue
Succasunna, NJ 07876
973-927-3971
wilowone@webtv.net
Public; by appointment;
seven-circuit classical, earth lined
with rock, outdoor, permanent
Completed: August 1997

Al's Nursery
Contact: Albert Compoly
1858 New Bedford Road
Wall Township, NJ 07719
732-449-4232
Private; call for availability;
painted concrete, outdoor, permanent

**Rising Phoenix Workshops and
  Retreats**
Built by: Kem Monk
Contact: Kem Monk
4 Skytop Road
Andover, NJ 07821
973-770-1096
RisingPhoenix@monmouth.com
Private; call for availability;
canvas, indoor, portable

Xavier Center
Contact: Diane Leffler
Convent Road
Convent Station, NJ 07691
973-290-5100
Private; call for availability;
canvas, indoor, portable

Institute of Core Energetics
291 Witherspoon Street
Princeton, NJ 08542
609-924-6863
Private; call for availability;
canvas, indoor, portable

NEW MEXICO

Public Labyrinth
Built by: Sonia Hodson and Bill
Enoch
Contact: Sonia Hodson or Bill
Enoch
Country Road 159
Abiquiu, NM 87510
(Labyrinth is across the road op-
posite the last house on the
right: #66, two-story)
505-685-4749
Public; always available; out-
door, seven-circuit Cretan, earth
and river stones
Completed: 1996

Private Labyrinth
Built by: Bob and Marge
McCarthy
Contact: Bob or Marge McCarthy
858 Camino Francisca
Santa Fe, NM 87501
505-989-8231
bobmarge@santfe.newmexico.
com
Semipublic; call for directions and availability; Chartres

pattern, river stones buried "on
end" in dirt
Completed: Fall 1999

Frenchy's Field
Contact: Emily Jacobson
Interfaith Council
Osage and Agua Fria
Santa Fe, NM 27501
505-983-3929
ruitkin@hotmail.com
Public; always available;
adobe mud, straw, wood, and
stone
Completed: August 1998

Museum of International Folk Art
Built by: The Labyrinth Resource
Group of Santa Fe
Contact: Marge McCarthy
Museum of International Folk Art
706 Camino Lejo
Santa Fe, NM 87504-2087
505-989-8231
bobmarge@santafe.newmexico.
com
Public; available daytimes;
Chartres, black cement and ob-
sidian
Completed: June 1999

Ghost Ranch Conference Center
Built by: Ghost Ranch Confer-
ence Center
Contact: Jean Richardson
HC 77 Box 11
Abiquiu, NM 87510
505-685-4333

ghostranch@cybermesa.com
Public; outdoor, available any time class is not in session; Chartres, flagstone and gravel
Completed: 1997

NEW YORK

Riverside Church
490 Riverside Drive
New York, NY 10027
212-870-6700
Public; open most Tuesday nights, 6 P.M. to 9 P.M., indoor, 30 ft., canvas

Union Square Park
Built by: Diana Carulli
17th Street (between Broadway and Park Ave.)
New York, NY
Public; open Tuesdays, Thursdays, Sundays, and occasional Mondays; outdoor, 40 ft., painted on asphalt, eleven-circuit, also seven-circuit Cretan

Spring Hollow
Built by: Paul Spring
Contact: Paul Spring
3595 Military Rd.
Newport, NY 13416
315-845-8998
Pnspring@aol.com

Semipublic; always available; stones, corn planted between the stones
Completed: 1999

Institute of Core Energetics
Contact: Barbara S. Arthur
115 East 23rd Street, 12th Floor
New York, NY 10010
212-505-6767
Private; call for availability; canvas, indoor, portable

Judson Memorial Church
Contact: Mary Ann Brussat
55 Washington Square South
New York, NY 10012
212-477-0351
Private; open for scheduled events; canvas, indoor, portable

D. M. Carulli Studio
Contact: Diana Carulli
73 Van Dam
New York, NY 10013
212-366-9424
Private; call for availability; outdoor, portable

Labyrinth Works
Contact: Elizabeth McGowan
P.O. Box 1288
New York, NY 10025
212-678-6750
Private, call for availability; canvas, indoor, portable

Westchester Medical Center
Contact: Polly Goodwin
Macy Oval
Valhalla, NY 10595
914-493-7125
Public; always open; grass, outdoor, permanent

"Falling Waters" Dominican Retreat Center
Built by: Helen Curry
Contact: Sister Mary Reynolds
43 Spaulding Lane
Saugerties, NY 12477
914-359-6400, ext. 215
Public; call for availability; brick, outdoor, permanent

Dominican Center
Built by: Helen Curry
Contact: Sister Mary Reynolds
175 Route 340
Sparkill, NY 10976
914-359-6400, Ext. 215
Public; call for availability; stone, outdoor, permanent

St. Ann's Church
Built by: Helen Curry
Contact: The Rev. Martha Overall
295 St. Ann's Avenue
Bronx, NY 10454
718-585-5632
Semipublic; available when churchyard is open; painted on paved playground, permanent

Stony Point Center
Contact: Rev. William Pinder
17 Crickettown Road
Stony Point, NY 10980-3299
914-786-5674
　　Private; call for availability;
outdoor, permanent

Garden of One
Contact: Ginther Rachel
246 CR 351
Medusa, NY 12120
518-239-8424
　　Private; call for availability;
outdoor, permanent

V.A. Medical Center
Contact: Harold Denkers
113 Holland Avenue
Albany, NY 12208
518-462-3311, ext. 2778
　　Public; always open; outdoor,
permanent

Mother Tree
Contact: Ellen Weaver
Woodstock, NY 12498
914-679-9706
　　Private; call for availability;
outdoor, permanent

Boughton Place
Contact: Clare Danielsson
150 Kisor Road
Highland, NY 12528
914-691-7578

Private; open for scheduled
events; outdoor, permanent

Burlingham Inn
Contact: Beth Bley
29 Vinegar Hill Road
Pine Bush, NY 12566
914-744-8499
　　Private; call for availability;
outdoor, permanent

**Turtle Walk at Foxglove Bed &
　Breakfast**
Contact: Suzanne Hoback
28 Main Street
Freeville, NY 13068
888-436-8608
　　Public; always open; outdoor,
permanent

Sacred Labyrinth at Spirit Lodge
Contact: Bert Prohaska
620 Brooks Road
Castle Creek, NY 13744
607-648-9758
　　Private; call for availability;
outdoor, permanent

Private Labyrinth
Contact: Donna and Skip
LaDuque
123 Biltmore Drive
Rochester, NY 14617
716-467-0704
　　Private; always open; out-
door, permanent

Wisdom's Goldenrod Center
Contact: David Gallagher
5801 Route 414
Hector, NY 14841
607-387-5863
　　Private; always open;
outdoor, grass, permanent

Foundation of Light
Contact: Mary Gilliland
399 Turkey Hill Road
Ithaca, NY 14850
607-273-9550
　　Private; always open;
outdoor, grass, permanent

Finger Lakes Labyrinths
Contact: David Gallagher
4421 West Semeca Road
Trumansburg, NY 14886
607-387-5863
　　Private; always open; grass,
outdoor, permanent

Judi and Lou Gurley
Built by: Marty Cain
1076 Fairport Rd.
Fairport, NY 14450
716-383-8585
　　Public; seven-path classical,
earthen with grass and flowers,
outdoor, permanent
　　Completed: 1992

Wainwright House
Built by: Helen Linz
Contact: Pat Tocci or Helen Linz

260 Stuyvesant Avenue
Rye, NY 10580
914-967-6080
  Semipublic; call for appointment; made of rounds of tree wood
  Completed: 2000

Mariondale Center
Built by: Al Mazza
Contact: Liz Molinari
299 North Highland Avenue
Ossining, NY 10562
914-941-4455
  Semipublic; call for appointment; brick walls, crushed stone path, seven-circuit
  Completed: 1999

NORTH CAROLINA

Mountain Valley Center
Contact: Jill and Charlie Henry
10248 Georgia Road
Otto, NC 28763
888-773-2491
www.mountainvalleycenter.com/labyrint.htm
  Public; open year-round from dawn to dusk, available for groups with advance reservations; seven-circuit, Cretan-style, natural earth and stone, outdoor, permanent

The Labyrinth at Country Road
Built by: Ina Warren
Contact: Ina Warren

126 Country Road
Brevard, NC 28712
828-862-4079
wildwood3@citcom.net or
warreniw@brevard.edu
  Semipublic; call for availability; 50 ft., Chartres-style, grass and inlaid brick, outdoor, permanent
  Completed: December 1999

Raleigh Arboretum
Built by: Marty Cain
Contact: Kim Wise
4301 Beryl Rd.
Raleigh, NC 27695
  Public; always open; seven-path classical, 60 ft., marked with flagstone paths, outdoor, permanent
  Completed: April 1996

The Labyrinth Center
58 Dark Star Way
Fairview, NC 28730
Labyrinthkeepers@worldnet.att.net
  Seven-circuit Cretan labyrinth

Winston-Salem Labyrinth Project
Contact: Polly Stern
P.O. Box 15052
Winston-Salem, NC 27113
910-722-7775
  Private; call for availability; canvas, indoor, portable

Holistic Center for Creative Renewal
Contact: Barbara Tazewell

600 Sunset Avenue
Asheboro, NC 27203
910-625-0846
  Public; open for scheduled events; canvas, indoor, portable

Holy Trinity Episcopal Church
Contact: Tim Patterson
607 North Green Street
Greensboro, NC 27401
336-272-6149
  Public; open for scheduled events; canvas, indoor, portable

Angels Nest Farm and Labyrinth
Contact: Dorothy Booth
585 Walnut Grove Road
Oxford, NC 27565
919-693-3229
angelbooth@gloryroad.net
  Private; open weekends from noon to 6 P.M., other by appointment; brick and mulch, outdoor, permanent

Sharon W. Warren, BCD, CCSW
Contact: Sharon Warren
505 Oberlin Road, Suite 148
Raleigh, NC 27609
919-467-3250
  Private; call for availability; seed kit, indoor, portable

The Haden Institute
Contact: Bob Haden
1819 Lyndhurst Ave.
Charlotte, NC 28203-5103
704-333-6058

Public; open for scheduled events; canvas, indoor, portable

Church of the Servant
Contact: Janet Carey and Jan Christopherson
4925 Oriole Drive
Wilmington, NC 28401
910-395-0616
Public; open for scheduled events; seed kit, indoor, portable

Road's End Retreat Center
Contact: Dottie Agnello
381 Road's End
Fleetwood, NC 28626
336-887-4640
Private; call for availability; grass, outdoor, permanent

Valle Crucis Conference Center
Contact: Jeanne Finan
P.O. Box 654
Valle Crucis, NC 28691
828-963-4453
Public; open for scheduled events; canvas, indoor, portable

In Spirit Resource
Contact: Robert and Elizabeth Libbey
123 Fork Creek Road
Saluda, NC 28773
828-749-3636
Private; call for availability; canvas, indoor, portable

St. Eugene Catholic Church
Contact: Rev. Francis Cancro
72 Culvern Street
Ashville, NC 28804
828-254-5193
Private; call for availability; canvas, indoor, portable

Pine Straw Labyrinth of the Great Mother
Built by: Lucy Oliver
Contact: Lucy Oliver
Dunbarton Development
Durham, NC 27701
919-490-8634
lucy.oliver@juno.com
Public; call for availability; seven-circuit classical, pine straw, outdoor
Completed: May 1999

St. Philip's Community Labyrinth
Built by: Lucy Oliver and others
Contact: St. Philip's Church
403 E. Main Street
Durham, NC 27701
919-682-5708
ahenrich@juno.com
Public; available all the time; 73-ft.-diameter Chartres-style, natural materials
Completed: December 1999

Public Labyrinth
Built by: Jeanette Stokes and others
Contact: Jeanette Stokes
1202 Watts Street

Durham, NC 27701
919-683-1236
StokesNet@aol.com
Public; call for availability; 40-ft.-diameter Chartres-style, canvas
Completed: Summer 1997

OHIO

Heritage Presbyterian Church
10425 Lebanon Pike
Centerville, OH 45458
513-885-5859

Trinity Cathedral
2021 East 22nd St.
Cleveland, OH 44115
216-771-3630, ext. 109

First Baptist Church
Contact: Judith Thomas
115 West Broadway
Granville, OH 43023
juditht@nextek.net
Public; open for scheduled events; canvas, indoor, portable

Universal Light Expo
Contact: Linda Cortellesi
P.O. Box 14246
Columbus, OH 43214
614-846-1882
Public; open for scheduled events; canvas, indoor, portable

Corpus Christi University Parish
Contact: Tom Puszczewicz
2955 Dorr St.
Toledo, OH 43607
tpuszcz@uoft02.edu
Public; available during church hours; canvas, indoor, portable

Collingwood Presbyterian Church
Contact: Bernie Wilhelm
2108 Collingwood Avenue
Toledo, OH 43620
419-243-3275
Public; open for scheduled events; canvas, indoor, portable

Private Labyrinth
Contact: Timothy Dodds
1093 Elm Street
Painesville, OH 44077
440-352-7557
Private; call for availability; outdoor, permanent

Trinity Cathedral
Contact: Trinity Cathedral
2021 East 22nd Street
Cleveland, OH 44115-2489
216-771-3630
Public; call for availability; canvas, indoor, portable

St. Joseph Christian Life Center
Contact: Andrea McGovern and Patricia Kassay
18485 Lake Shore Blvd.
Cleveland, OH 44119

216-531-7370, ext. 115 or 122
Public; call for availability; canvas, indoor, portable

Ursuline Sophia Center
Contact: Lucretia Bohnsack
2600 Lander Road
Pepper Pike, OH 44124
sophictr@apk.net
Public; available the second Tuesday of each month—9 A.M. to 8 P.M.; canvas, indoor, portable

Crown Point Ecology Center
Contact: Donna Bessken
3220 Ira Road
Bath, OH 44210
330-666-9200
Public; call for availability; grass, outdoor, permanent

Private Labyrinth
Contact: Lynette McCormack
8410 Darlene Drive
West Chester, OH 45069
513-759-2091
Private; open for scheduled events; grass, outdoor, permanent

Health Re-Source Center
Contact: Michael Klosterman
6914 Paxton Road
Loveland, OH 45140
513-683-2849
Private; call for availability; outdoor, permanent

Northern Hills Fellowship Unitarian Universalist Church
Contact: Linda Neumaier
460 Fleming Road
Cincinnati, OH 45231-4054
513-771-0915
Public; always open; grass, outdoor, permanent

Celebration of Life
Contact: Andy Hock
4100 Benfield Road
Dayton, OH 45429
colcsom@erinct.com
Public; open for scheduled events; canvas, indoor, portable

Farmelot
Contact: Stephanie Vradelis
27696 Locust Grove Road
McArthur, OH 45651
740-596-0221
Public; call for availability; rock or garden, outdoor, permanent

Walking Meditation
Contact: Suzanne Trautwein
454 Scarlet Oak Dr.
Findlay, OH 45840
419-423-8620
Private; call for availability; indoor, portable

OREGON

Trinity Episcopal Cathedral
Contact: Sally Newlands
147 NW 19th Avenue
Portland, Oregon 97209
503-222-9911, Fax: 503-294-
7069
Public; call for availability;
canvas, indoor, portable

Ashland Friends of the Labyrinth
Contact: Betty Hutto
P.O. Box 615
Ashland, OR 97520
541-482-6422
BettyHutto@aol.com
Eleven-circuit, 37-ft.
diameter, canvas, portable

Public Labyrinth
Built by: Robert Ferré
Contact: Andy Telynor Andrews
38536 Scravel Hill Rd. NE
Albany, OR 97321
541-327-3573
hobbit@proaxis.com
Public; by appointment,
workshops
Completed: September 1999

Lincoln City Labyrinth
Built by: Robert Ferré, St. Louis
Labyrinth Project
Contact: Mary Flannery
Congregational Church
1760 NW 2th St.

Lincoln City, OR 97367
541-994-2378
congregational@wcn.net
Semipublic; available on the
last Tuesday of each month from
4 P.M. to 8 P.M.; canvas
Completed: August 1999

PENNSYLVANIA

**The Common Ground Labyrinth
    Project**
Built by: Carol Posch Comstock,
Cheryl Lossie, Robert Ferré, and
the St. Louis Labyrinth Project
Contact: Carol Posch Comstock
or Cheryl Lossie
Erie, PA
814-899-6453 or 814-734-4610
spiritoes@aol.com
Semipublic; currently,
monthly walks are held at Mercy-
hurst; Chartres-style labyrinth,
36-ft. diameter, canvas
Completed: November 1997

**The Blessing Seed Labyrinth
(see The Common Ground
Labyrinth Project** for contact information)
Semipublic; limited availability; seven-circuit classical; canvas,
portable
Completed: January 2000

Bryn Mawr College Labyrinth
Built by: Jeanne-Rachel Salomon
and Robert Burton
Contact: Robert Burton, Director
of Grounds and College Horticul-
turist
101 North Merion Avenue
Bryn Mawr, PA 19010-2899
610-526-7938
rburton@brynmawr.edu
Semipublic; always available
for individuals, call for group
availability; turf and mulch, outdoor
Completed: Fall 1998

St. Stephen's Episcopal Church
19 South Tenth Street
Philadelphia, PA 19107
215-922-3807
ststevepa@aol.com

CCAC—South Campus
Contact: David Woolf
1750 Clairton Rd.
West Mifflin, PA 15122-3029
412-469-62224
Public; always open; outdoor,
permanent

East Liberty Presbyterian Church
Contact: Rev. Hydie Houston
116 South Highland Avenue
Pittsburgh, PA 15206
412-441-3800
Public; open for scheduled
events; canvas, indoor, portable

St. Mark's Episcopal Church
Contact: Annis Rogers
335 Locust Street
Johnstown, PA 15901
814-535-6797
Public; always open; outdoor, permanent

Sisters of the Humility of Mary
Contact: Kathleen Perry
Villa Maria Community Center
Villa Maria, PA 16155
724-964-8920, Ext. 3348
Private; call for availability; grass, outdoor, permanent

Therapeutic Bodywork, Inc.
Contact: Sandra M. Snyder
1449 Willowbrook Drive
Boalsburg, PA 16827
814-466-3353
Public; always open; outdoor, permanent

Great Conewago Presbyterian Church
Contact: Betty Neely
174 Red Bridge Road
Gettysburg, PA 17325
717-334-7718
Public; always open; indoor, permanent

Lehigh Valley Labyrinth Project
Contact: Linda A. Toggart
724 First Ave.
Bethlehem, PA 18018
610-882-2359

Public; open for scheduled events; canvas, indoor, portable

Covenant Presbyterian Church
Contact: JoAnn Germerhausen
550 Madison Ave.
Scranton, PA 18510
570-346-6400
Public; call for availability; canvas, indoor, portable

SOUTH CAROLINA

St. Martin's in the Field
Contact: Judy Tighe
5220 Clemson Avenue
Columbia, SC 29206
803-782-8686
Public; open for scheduled events; canvas, indoor, portable

Private Labyrinth
Contact: Thomas Pola
3832 Gates Ford Rd.
Kershaw, SC 29067
803-475-75421
Private; open for scheduled events; garden, outdoor, permanent

Hospice of the Upstate
Contact: Betty Blackerby
Rogers Road
Anderson, SC 29601
864-224-2015

Public; always open; outdoor, permanent

Holy Cross Episcopal Church
Contact: Dana Bunting
205 E. College Street
Simpsonville, SC 29681
864-967-7470
Public; two labyrinths available, call for availability; canvas, indoor, portable, and outdoor, permanent

Innana
Built by: Marcy Walsh
Contact: Marcy Walsh
414 Country Club Blvd.
Summerville, SC 29483
843-873-1113
mswalsh@awod.com
Semipublic; call for arrangements; seven-circuit classical, grass and stones, outdoor, permanent
Completed: December 1998

TENNESSEE

Church of the Redeemer
101 April Lane
Shelbyville, TN 37160
615-684-5506

St. Mark's Episcopal Church
Contact: Scott Lee
3100 Murfreesboro Pike
Antioch, TN 37013
614-361-4100

Public; always open; grass, outdoor, permanent

Crosswinds Contemplative Center
Contact: Lucy H. Morgan
6923 Cross Keys Road
College Grove, TN 37046
615-368-7525
Public; call for availability; outdoor, permanent

Buckhorn Inn
Contact: Lee Mellor
2140 Tudor Mountain Road
Gatlinburg, TN 37738
423-436-4668
Public; available 6 A.M. to 8 P.M.; eleven-circuit, 60 ft., rock or garden, outdoor, permanent

Private Labyrinth
Contact: Caroline Munday
905 Glennshire
Knoxville, TN 37923
423-531-7504
Private; always open; canvas, indoor, portable

Lindenwood Christian Church
Contact: Rev. Owen Guy
2400 Union Avenue
Memphis, TN 38112
901-458-8506
Public; call for availability; canvas, indoor, portable

Patty and Steven Silver
Built by: Marty Cain
1948 Riversound Dr.
Knoxville, TN 37922
615-966-7541
Public; seven-path classical marked with stones, permanent
Completed: March 1997

TEXAS

The Unity Church of Dallas
Contact: John Barnes
6611 Forest Lane
Dallas, TX 75230
972-233-7106
http://www.unitydallas.org
Public; open seven days a week, 24 hours per day, except from about 10:30 on Sunday morning to about 1:00 Sunday afternoon; outdoor, paint on asphalt; two labyrinths, a circular form and a hexagonal form
Completed: 1998

Bishop Quarterman Conference Center
232 East Cottonwood
Amarillo, TX 79108
2201 Civic Circle, #315
806-383-6878
ricck@aol.com
Public; brick and grass, outdoor

All Saints' Episcopal Church
Contact: The Labyrinth Committee
3026 South Staples
Corpus Christi, Texas 78404
512-879-4071

Episcopal Church of the Transfiguration
14115 Hillcrest Road
Dallas, TX 75240-8699
972-233-1898

Emmanuel Episcopal Church
3 South Randolph Street
San Angelo, TX 76903
915-653-2446
eec@airmail.net

Lia Austin
Built by: Marty Cain
Contact: Diane Roman
1707 Aggie Lane
Austin, TX 78757
512-467-9128
Public; seven-path, permanent
Completed: April 1996

VERMONT

Lucy and Knox Cummin
Built by: Marty Cain
Box 13, Tower House
Huntington, VT 05462
802-434-3285

lucyavery@aol.com
Public; seven-path
Completed: June 1995

Solar Hill
Built by: Marty Cain
Contact: Elaine Johnson
61 Western Ave.
Brattleboro, VT 05301
802-254-6990
Public; seven-path classical, marked with stones, permanent
Completed: May 1997

Cindy Arseneau
Built by: Marty Cain
Manchester Center, VT 05255
802-326-0201
Public; seven-path classical, marked with stones, permanent
Completed: September 1999

Community Labyrinths
Built by: Judith Joyce and friends
Contact: Judith Joyce
4507 Main Street
Waitsfield, Vt 05673
802-496-9237
jmjoyce@spirit-matters.com
Semipublic; call for availability; eleven-circuit, Chartres-style, canvas; and seven-circuit, nylon
Completed: October 1996; April 1998

Triquetra
Contact: Cielle Tewksbury

R.R. 4, Box 114
Brattleboro, VT 05301
802-257-0183
Private; always open; outdoor, permanent

Manitou
Contact: Stewart McDermet
Butterfield Road
Dummerston, VT 05301
802-254-3555
Private; always open; grass, outdoor, permanent

First Universalist Parish
Contact: Jane Dwinell
Main Street
Derby Line, Vt 05830
802-754-8780 or 802-873-3563
Public; call for availability; canvas, outdoor, portable

Hardwick Chiropractic
Contact: Grace Johnstone
54 School Circle
East Hardwick, VT 05836
802-472-3033
Public; always open; outdoor, permanent

The People Barn Retreat Center
Built by: Lynn Shelton
Contact: Sally Lonegren
P.O. Box 125
Greensboro, VT 05841
802-533-2335
SLonegren@aol.com

Semipublic; by appointment; seven-path classical, marked with stones and flowers, permanent; Chartres-style, canvas; seven-circuit, grass, outdoor
Completed: 1998

VIRGINIA

St. Paul's Episcopal Church
Contact: The Rev. Dr. Vienna Cobb Anderson
815 East Grace Street
Richmond, VA 23219
804-643-3589
vcanderson@stpauls-episcopal.org
Public; call for availability; canvas eleven-circuit Chartres-style; also building five-circuit Hopi, and ancient seven-circuit Celtic labyrinths
Completed: August 1999

Blue Ridge Wellness Center
Contact: Patricia Henderson
RT 5, Box 171
Forest, VA 24551
804-525-1164
Public; 24 hours a day; seven-path classical, marked with stones and flowers, outdoor

A.R.E. Labyrinth (Association for Research and Enlightenment)
Built by: Meryl Ann Butler and volunteers

Contact: Meryl Ann Butler
Atlantic Avenue at 67th Street
Virginia Beach, VA 23451
757-428-3588
merylannb@aol.com
http://www.are-cayce.com
   Public; open 24 hours a day;
Chartres-style, 48-ft. diameter,
cement paint on patio, outdoor,
permanent
   Completed: April 1998

Warrenton United Methodist Church

Contact: Mamie Gray
231 Church Street
Warrenton, VA 20186
540-347-9415
   Public; call for availability;
outdoor, permanent

Burke Presbyterian Church

Contact: Jeanne Bolick
5690 Oak Leather Drive
Burke, VA 22015
703-323-9448
   Public; open for scheduled
events; canvas, indoor, portable

King of Kings Lutheran Church

Contact: Judi Hangen
4025 Kings Way
Fairfax, VA 22033
703-378-7272
   Public; call for availability;
canvas, indoor, portable

The Labyrinth Project of the Unitarian Universalist Church of Arlington, VA

Built by: The Labyrinth Project
Committee
Contact: Jane Anthony-Buckman
4444 Arlington Blvd.
Arlington, VA 22207
703-892-2565 (UUCA)
LabyrinthUUCA@wizard.net
   Public; regularly scheduled
walks; eleven-circuit, Chartres-
style, 42-ft. diameter, canvas
   Completed: 1995

The Lord's Chapel

Contact: Suwahlu Adams
Winchester, VA 22637
540-667-7737
   Public; always open; outdoor,
permanent

Thomas Jefferson Memorial Unitarian Universalist Church

Contact: Leia Durland-Jones
717 Rugby Road
Charlottesville, VA 22903
804-293-8179
   Public; open for scheduled
events; canvas, indoor, portable

The Chrysalis Group at Union Theological Seminary

Contact: William Arnold
P.O. Box 7069
Richmond, VA 23221
804-355-9751
   Public; always open; outdoor,
permanent

River Road Church

Contact: Robert Dibble
8000 River Road
Richmond, VA 23229-8415
804-288-1131
   Public; open for scheduled
events; canvas, indoor, portable

Grace Episcopal Church

Contact: Jean Kirkham
111 Church Street, P.O. Box 123
Yorktown, VA 23690
757-898-3261
   Public; call for availability;
seed kit, indoor, portable

King of Kings Labyrinth

Built by: Robert Ferré
Contact: Judi Hangen
King of Kings Lutheran Church
4025 Kings Way
Fairfax, VA 22033
703-378-7272
hanghome@worldnet.att.net
   Open to the public at specific
times; check schedule at:
www.kofk.org; painted canvas,
Chartres eleven-circuit design,
35 ft.
   Completed: October 1998

Shenandoah Labyrinth

Built by: Miki Leeper
Contact: Miki Leeper
323 S. Buckton Rd.
Middletown, VA 22645
polaris@shentel.net

Currently open monthly on the first Friday of the month at the First Presbyterian Church in Winchester; eleven-circuit labyrinth is available for use in other sites. 31 ft. wide

Completed: September 1998

WASHINGTON, D.C.

Church of the Epiphany
1317 G Street N.W.
Washington, DC 20005
202-347-2635
Public; call for availability; canvas, indoor, portable

WISCONSIN

St. Ann's Church and Healing Sanctuary
Contact: Pastor Gary Wright
5933 W. National Avenue
West Allis, WI 53214
414-259-1229
Public; call for availability; canvas, indoor, portable

Madison Christian Community Church
Contact: Sonja Keesey-Berg
7118 Old Sauk Road
Madison, WI 53717-1099
608-836-1455

Public; two labyrinths available, call for availability; grass, outdoor, permanent

Sinsinawa Mound
Contact: Janice DeMuth
County Road Z
Sinsinawa, WI 53824-9999
608-748-4411, ext. 811
Public; two labyrinths available, always open; canvas, indoor, portable; and outdoor, permanent

Servants of Mary Convent
Contact: Nancy Wheeler
1000 College Avenue W.
Ladysmith, WI 54848
715-532-9611
Public; always open; grass, outdoor, portable

First Congregational Church
Contact: Jane Weeden
724 E. South River St.
Appleton, WI 54915
920-733-7393
Public; call for availability; canvas, indoor, portable

CANADA

Bells Corners United Church
Contact: Ruth Richardson
3955 Richmond Rd.
Nepean, Ontario K2H 5C5
613-828-2155

St. Paul's Anglican Church, Westdale
Contact: Kate Snider
1140 King Street West
Hamilton, Ontario L8S 1M1
905-528-3724
bobvanes@netaccess.on.ca
Public; guided walks monthly (third Thursday evenings at 7:30), also by appointment; eleven-circuit, painted on the parish hall floor, permanent

Kebec Crystal Mines
Built by: Marty Cain
Contact: Gaudry and Priscella Norman
430 11e Rang, Bonsecours
Quebec, Canada J0E 1H0
514-535-6550
Public; by appointment; seven-path classical, white quartz crystal, permanent; French spoken
Completed: 1991

Maria Hager
Built by: Marty Cain
Uigg Vernon Bridge
Prince Edward Island, Canada C0A 2E0
902-651-2302
By appointment; small seven-path labyrinth, marked with sticks and string, permanent
Completed: 1995

RECOMMENDED RESOURCES

LABYRINTH BOOKS

Artress, Lauren. *Walking a Sacred Path: Rediscovering the Labyrinth as a Sacred Tool.* New York: Riverhead Books, 1995.

Attali, Jacques. *Labyrinth in Culture and Society: Pathways to Wisdom.* English translation (from the French) by Joseph H. Rowe. Berkeley, CA.: North Atlantic Books, 1999. Original French publication: *Chemins de Sagesse.* Fayard, 1996. Color photos and illustrations.

Bartnett, Beatrice. *Peace Labyrinth: Sacred Geometry.* Ruidoso, N.M.: Lifestyle Institute, 1995.

Burckhardt, Titus. *Chartres and the Birth of the Cathedral.* Translated from the German by William Stoddart. Foreword by Keith Critchlow. Ipswich, UK: Golgonooza Press, 1996. First published in German by Urs Graf Verlag, 1962. Published in United States by World Wisdom Books, Bloomington, Ind.

Champion, Alex B. *Earth Mazes.* Self-published by the author, 1990. Champion@zapcom.net; Voice: 707-895-3375; Fax: 707-895-2598; or P.O. Box 145, Philo, CA 95466.

Doob, Penelope Reed. *The Idea of the Labyrinth from Classical Antiquity through the Middle Ages.* Ithaca, N.Y.: Cornell University Press, 1990.

Ferré, Robert. *The Labyrinth Revival.* St. Louis: One Way Press (publishing division of the St. Louis Labyrinth Project), 1996. Self-published and available from the author: Robert Ferré, St. Louis Labyrinth Project, 128 Slocum Avenue, St. Louis, MO 63198. Voice: 314-968-5557; Fax (USA): 314-968-5539.

————. *How to Make a 7-Circuit Labyrinth.* St. Louis: One Way Press, 1997. For ordering information, please see preceding citation.

————. *The Chartres Labyrinth Trilogy.* St. Louis: One Way Press, 1997.

Fisher, Adrian, and Howard Loxton. *Secrets of the Maze: An Interactive Guide to the World's Most Amazing Mazes.* London: Thames and Hudson, 1997.

Goldstein, Lisa. *Walking the Labyrinth.* New York: Tor Press, 1996.

Gutierrez, Donald. *The Maze in the Mind and the World: Labyrinths in Modern Literature.* Troy, NY: Whitston Publishing Company, 1985.

Hooke, S. H. *The Labyrinth: Further Studies in the Relation between Myth and Ritual in the Ancient World.* London: Society for Promoting Christian Knowledge; New York: Macmillan, 1935.

Jaskolski, Helmut. *The Labyrinth: Symbol of Fear, Rebirth, and Liberation.* Translated by Michael H. Kohn. Boston:

Shambhala Publications, 1997. Original German edition, Stuttgart: Kreuz Verlag, 1994.

Lockridge, Ross. F. *The Labyrinth of New Harmony.* New Harmony, Ind.: New Harmony Memorial Commission, 1941. Reprint, Westport, Conn.: Hyperion Press, 1975.

Lonegren, Sig. *Labyrinths: Ancient Myths and Modern Uses.* Somerset, England: Gothic Image Publications, 1991; 2nd rev. ed., 1996.

Matthews, W. H. *Mazes and Labyrinths: Their History and Development.* London: Longmans, Green, and Co., 1922. Dover edition, first published in 1970; reprinted 1985.

Pennick, Nigel. *Mazes and Labyrinths.* London: Robert Hale, 1990.

Querido, René. *The Golden Age of Chartres.* Hudson, N.Y.: Anthroposophical Press, 1987.

Saward, Jeff. *Ancient Labyrinths of the World.* Booklet published by *Caerdroia: The Journal of Mazes and Labyrinths,* 1997. *Caerdroia,* 53 Thundersley Grove, Thundersley, Essex, England SS7-3EB.

Shields, Carol. *Larry's Party.* New York: Viking Press, 1997; Penguin USA, 1998.

Taylor, Jeremy. *The Living Labyrinth: Exploring Universal Themes in Myths, Dreams, and the Symbolism of Waking Life.* New York: Paulist Press, 1998.

Torrez, Kay. *Labyrinths: What Are They? Prehistory to the 21st Century.* Phoenix: Labyrinths Unlimited, 1994.

West, Melissa Gayle. *Exploring the Labyrinth: A Guide for Healing and Spiritual Growth.* N.Y.: Broadway Books, 2000.

BOOKS FOR THE JOURNEY

Anderson, Sherry Ruth. *The Feminine Face of God: The Unfolding of the Sacred in Women.* Patricia Hopkins, contributor. N.Y.: Bantam Doubleday Dell, 1992.

Auel, Jean M. *Clan of the Cave Bear.* N.Y.: Bantam Books, 1994.

Bolen, Jean Shinoda. *Crossing to Avalon: A Woman's Midlife Pilgrimage.* San Francisco: Harper San Francisco, 1995.

Bradley, Marion Zimmer. *The Mists of Avalon.* N.Y.: Del Rey, 1987.

Cameron, Julia. *Artist's Way.* N.Y.: J. P. Tarcher, 1995.

Carroll, Lee. *Kyron—the End Times: New Information for Personal Peace (Kyron Book 1).* San Diego: Kyron Writings, 1993.

——————. *Kyron—Don't Think Like a Human: Channelled Answers to Basic Questions (Kyron Book 2).* San Diego: Kyron Writings, 1994.

——————. *Alchemy of the Human Spirit: A Guide to Human Transition into the New Age (Kyron Book 3).* San Diego: Kyron Writings, 1995.

Estes, Clarissa Pinkola. *Women Who Run with the Wolves: Myths and Stories of the Wild Woman Archetype.* N.Y.: Ballantine Books, 1995.

Haddon, Genia Pauli. *Uniting Sex, Self and Spirit: Let the Body Be Your Guide to New Consciousness and Deeper Spirituality in a Changing Age.* Scotland, CT.: Plus Publications/Helix, 1993.

Haich, Elizabeth. *Initiation.* Palo Alto, CA.: Seed Center, 1994.

Hartmann, Thom. *The Last Hours of Ancient Sunlight: Waking Up to Personal & Global Transformation.* N.Y.: Harmony Books, 1998.

Kabat-Zinn, Jon. *Wherever You Go There You Are.* N.Y.: Hyperion, 1995.

Kidd, Sue Monk. *The Dance of the Dissident Daughter: A Woman's Journey from the Christian Tradition to the Sacred Feminine.* San Francisco: Harper San Francisco, 1996.

Kinstler, Clysta. *The Moon Under Her Feet.* San Francisco: Harper San Francisco, 1991.

Marciniak, Barbara. *Bringers of the Dawn: Teachings from the Pliadians.* Edited by Tera L. Thomas. Santa Fe, N.M.: Bear & Co., 1992.

Morgan, Marlo. *Mutant Message Down Under.* N.Y.: HarperCollins, 1995.

Myss, Caroline. *Anatomy of the Spirit: The Seven Stages of Power and Healing.* N.Y.: Random House, 1997.

Rodegast, Pat. *Emmanuel's Book: A Manual for Living Comfortably in the Cosmos.* Judith Stanton, contributor. N.Y.: Bantam Books, 1987.

———. *Emmanuel's Book II: The Choice for Love (New Age).* Introduction by Ram Dass. N.Y.: Bantam Doubleday Dell, 1989.

———. *Emmanuel's Book III: What Is an Angel Doing Here?* Edited by Judith Stanton. N.Y.: Bantam Doubleday Dell, 1994.

Starbird, Margaret. *The Woman with the Alabaster Jar: Mary Magdalen and the Holy Grail.* Introduction by Terance A. Sweeney. Santa Fe, N.M.: Bear & Co., 1993.

Walsch, Neale Donald. *Conversations with God: An Uncommon Dialogue (Book One).* N.Y.: Putnam Publishing Group, 1996.

———. *Conversations with God: An Uncommon Dialogue (Book Two).* Charlottesville, VA.: Hampton Roads Publishing Co., 1997.

———. *Conversations with God: An Uncommon Dialogue (Book Three).* Charlottesville, VA.: Hampton Roads Publishing Co., 1997.

———. *Friendship with God: An Uncommon Dialogue.* N.Y.: G. P. Putnam & Sons, 1999.

PERIODICALS

Caerdroia: The Journal of Mazes and Labyrinths. Contact: Jeff Saward, editor (and founder), *Caerdroia*, 53 Thundersley Grove, Thunderseley, Essex, England SS7 3EB. Telphone: 011-44-1268-751915. E-mail: caerdroia@dial.pipex.com. Web site: http://www.labyrinthos.net. At the *Caerdroia* World Wide Web site, there is a complete listing of all the articles that have appeared in *Caerdroia* since its inception in 1980.

Labyrinthian: Journeys of the Spirit Newsletter. Contact: *Labyrinthian*, P.O. Box 40303, Pittsburgh, PA 15201. E-mail: violin@nb.net.

VIDEOS

Building Labyrinths on the Earth for Spiritual and Physical Well-Being, with Marty Cain. Produced and narrated by Marty Cain, 1995. Approximate running time: 60 minutes. To order, write or call: Park Street Studio, 55 Park Street, Newport, NH 03773. Telephone: 603-863-7343. E-mail: marty@sugar-river.com.

Dance of the Labyrinth. Produced by Kelley Ellesworth, 1998. Running time: available in two versions, 21 minutes and 11 minutes. To order, write or call: Sandra Wasko-Flood, 8106 Norwood Drive, Alexandria, VA 22309. Telephone: 703-360-5233. E-mail: Ekim-Doolf@erols.com.

Journeys into Healing—"*The Labyrinth*," Parts 1 and 2, featuring Dr. Wayne London, M.D. Wisdom Network Productions, 1999. Running time (each part): 30 minutes (shows 1264 and 1265). To order, write or call: Wisdom Network, P.O. Box 1546, Bluefield, WV 24701. Telephone: 888-694-7366. Fax: 304-589-7252. Web site: www.wisdomnetwork.com.

Labyrinth: The History of the Maze, with master maze designer and builder Adrian Fisher and interview segments with the Rev. Lauren Artress. New River Media Productions, 1996. Approximate running time: 60 minutes. To order, telephone: 202-775-4945.

Labyrinths: Their Mystery and Magic, with Richard Feather Anderson, Jeff Saward, and Robert Ferré. Produced by Penny Price, 1997. Approximate running time: 60 minutes. Taped at the 1996 Labyrinth Conference, Omega Institute, Rhinebeck, N.Y. To order, write or call: Penny Price Media, 63 Mountain View Road, Rhinebeck, NY 12572. Telephone: 914-876-0239. Fax: 914-876-0260.

Magic, Mystery and Miracles of the Labyrinth: The Rediscovery of an Ancient Tool for Personal Transformation. Aum Girl Productions, 1997. Running time: 81 minutes. To order, write or call: Aum Girl Productions, P.O. Box 1633, Los Angeles, CA 90066. Telephone: 310-392-7366.

Mazes & Labyrinths: The Search for the Center. Cyclone Productions, 1996.

Walking in Sacred Circles. The Labyrinth Project of Connecticut, Inc., 1993. Running time: 27 minutes. Documentary on the making of the Chartres labyrinth on canvas. To order, write or call: Helen Curry, P.O. Box 813, New Canaan, CT 06840. Telephone: 203-966-5459.

RECOMMENDED MUSIC FOR LABYRINTH WALKING

SACRED MUSIC

Chant. The Benedictine Monks of Santo Domingo de Silos. Angel Records, 1994

Chant Noel. The Benedictine Monks of Santo Domingo de Silos. Angel Records, 1994

Beyond Chant. Voices of Ascension. Delos International, 1994

Voices of Angels: Hildegard von Bingen. Voices of Ascension. Delos International, 1997

The Chant of Christmas Midnight. The Schola Cantorum of St. Peter's. Imaginery Road Records, 1995

Canticles of Ecstasy: Hildegard von Bingen. Sequentia. BMG Music, 1994

Symphoniae: Hildegard von Bingen. Sequentia. BMG Music, 1989

Vision: The Music of Hildegard von Bingen. Germaine Fritz and Emily Van Eveda. Angel Records, 1994

A Feather on the Breath of God: Hildegard von Bingen. Kirkby/Gothic Voices. Hyperion Records Ltd., 1984

Love's Illusion. Anonymous 4. Harmonia Mundi, 1994

Spem in Alium. Thomas Tallis. The Tallis Scholars. Gimell Records, 1985

SECULAR MUSIC

Music to Walk the Labyrinth. Richard Shulman. RichHeart Music, 1999

Keeper of the Holy Grail. Richard Shulman. RichHeart Music, 1997

Music for Magnified Healing. Richard Shulman. RichHeart Music, 1994

Eight String Religion. David Darling. Hearts of Space, 1993

Cello. David Darling. ECM Records, 1992

Wolf Eyes. Paul Winter. Living Music Records, 1988

Touch. Michael Jones. Narada Productions, 1996

The Silent Path. Robert Haig Coxon. R. H. C. Productions, 1995

The Music of Olympic National Park. Mars Lasar. Real Music, 1996

Circles of Discovery. Debbie Danbrook. Twilight Songs (SOSCAN), 1998

Canyon Trilogy. R. Carlos Nakai. Canyon Records Productions, 1989

Music from the Pleiades. Gerald Jay Markoe. Astromusic, 1989

LABYRINTH RESOURCES

The Labyrinth Project of Connecticut, Inc.
www.CTlabyrinth.org

Offers public walks on both the classical seven-circuit and the Chartres eleven-circuit labyrinths, and workshops are given by request. A three-circuit ceremonial labyrinth is available for weddings and other rituals. For more information contact: Helen Curry at 203-966-5121 or P.O. Box 813, New Canaan, CT 06840.

The Labyrinth Society
www.labyrinthsociety.org

The Labyrinth Society aims to support all those who create, maintain, and use labyrinths and to serve the global community by providing education, networking, and opportunities to experience transformation. Its members include many of the foremost experts and luminaries, and it holds conventions each year. There is an online discussion list linked to the site. Mail: P.O. Box 144, New Canaan, CT, 06840. Telephone: 877-446-4520.

Ashland WWWeb Services

www.ashlandweb.com/labyrinth

This southern Oregon Web community has chosen to use the labyrinth as the theme of its site. It has a Labyrinth of Human Development that includes an article on labyrinths as seen across culture and time and which has links to some useful resources.

Awakenings: Lessons for Living

www.lesons4living.com

There is a labyrinth section which includes labyrinth information, a free labyrinth screen saver, and the 3D Labyrinth Stereogram.

British Turf Labyrinths

www.indigogroup.co.uk/edge/index.htm

Covers all of the known earth mazes in Britain.

Caerdroia

www.labyrinthos.net

British labyrinth publication's Web site.

Earth Symbols

www.earthsymbols.com

Labyrinth builder Alex Champion describes the labyrinthine garden sculptures he creates and explains the spiritual and artistic ideas that shape them. Mail: P.O. Box 145, Philo, CA 95466. Telephone: 707-895-

3375; Fax: 707-895-2598; e-mail: Champion@zap com.net.

Georgia Labyrinths

www.avana.net/%7Ebpeach/georgialabyrinths.htm

Bob Peach provides information on labyrinths available to the public in the state of Georgia as well as thoughts and suggestions on walking a labyrinth on a spiritual level. Also included: an outline for blessing labyrinths and information on Taize services.

Golden Spirit

www.goldenspirit.com

Labyrinth jewelry. Mail: 2316 Pine Ridge Road, Naples, Florida 34109. Telephone: 941-566-9644.

Jo Edkin's Maze Page

www.gwydir.demon.co.uk/jo/maze/index.htm

A useful introduction to unicursal labyrinths with lots of clear diagrams, plus some elegant designs of her own.

The Labyrinth Company

www.labyrinthcompany.com

David Tolzmann builds labyrinths in your choice of design, colors and materials, custom-fitted for your particular space and your specific requirements. Mail: 175 Ninth Avenue, New York, NY 10011. Telephone: 212-337-9974; Fax: 212-645-8504.

Labyrinth Goods & Services

labyrinth.hypermart.net

Pamela Ramadei sells labyrinth products along with labyrinth workshops and seminars. Mail: 6056 Oberstrasse, Evergreen, Colorado 80439. Telephone: 303-670-9639; orders toll free 877-711-LABY (5229); e-mail: prama7@aol.com.

Labyrinthina
www.labyrinthina.com
 Kathy Doore has put together a lovely site on labyrinth spirituality, with emphasis on earth mysteries, energy, and dowsing. There are sections on the myth and mystery of labyrinths, relevant books, links, and personal experiences.

The Labyrinth Project of Alabama
www.geocities.com/Yosemite/6182/alalab.html
 Encourages and nurtures creative imagination, intuition, beauty, wholeness, connection, and healing through the labyrinth experience.

Labyrinth Work
www.labyrinthwork.com
 Labyrinth and labyrinth-related items. Mail: P.O. Box 7591, Arlington, VA 22207. Telephone: 703-524-3681; Fax: 703-524-2118.

Mid-Atlantic Geomancy
www.geomancy.org
 This site, run by Sig Lonegren and Patrick MacManaway, has lots of information about earth energies, archaeo-astronomy, sacred geometry, and dowsing. There is a whole section on labyrinths, including information about how to draw them, the names of the parts, their relationship to colors and chakras, and Lonegren's simple but effective labyrinth meditation technique.

Paxworks
www.paxworks.com
 Labyrinth products and services, a photo gallery, recommended books and CDs, workshop referral services.

Relax-4-Life
www.labyrinthproducts.com
 A full line of unique and affordable wood finger labyrinths, including the versatile two-handed/two-person Intuipath™, as well as other labyrinth products. Telephone: 847-842-1752; Fax: 847-842-1751; e-mail: relax4life@aol.com.

St. Louis Labyrinth Project
www.labyrinthproject.com
 This project is *"dedicated to reclaiming the use of the labyrinth, an ancient spiritual tool, through sponsoring events for labyrinth walking, promoting education and research about labyrinths, and placing labyrinths for public and private use."* It produces a wide range of information booklets, kits, and other materials. Mail: 128 Slocum Avenue, St. Louis, MO 63119. Telephone: 314-968-5557; Fax: 314-968-5539.

Through Mazes to Mathematics
www.math.sunysb.edu/%7Etony/mazes/index.html
 A look at labyrinths by Tony Phillips of the State University of New York. Of interest to those with a mathematical bent. Very interesting and different way of looking at these ancient tools.

Veriditas
www.gracecathedral.com/labyrinth/index.html
 Lauren Artress of Grace Cathedral in San Francisco is behind this comprehensive site, which includes a directory of mainly Christian-type labyrinths as well as lots of useful information.

A Web of Labyrinth
www.mcli.dist.maricopa.edu/smc/labyrinth
    Developed by a team of students and their mythology teacher, the site chronicles various labyrinth festivals at South Mountain Community College in California since 1994, plus a "gallery" of labyrinths from around the world and interactive activities for drawing a labyrinth and exploring the inner labyrinth.

    In addition to the sources above, two labyrinth builders who do not have Web sites deserve special mention:

Marty Cain
    Mail: 55 Park Street, Newport, NH 03773. Telephone: 603-863-7343. Can be reached via e-mail: marty@sugar-river.net.

Victoria Stone, MPH,
    Mail: 893 Noe Street, San Francisco, CA 94114. Telephone: 415-826-0904; Fax: 415-826-1893; email: vicstone@ix.netcom.com.

INDEX

Page numbers in *italics* refer to picture captions.

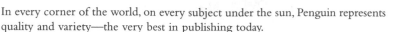